The Christian & Homosexuality

Understanding One of the Greatest Moral Challenges Faced by the Church

Charlie Avila

First published in the *Spirit of Wisdom & Revelation* newsletters and in the teacherofthebible.com website in the United States.

Clovis Christian Center
3606 N. Fowler Ave
Fresno, California, USA 93727-1124

Copyright © 2018 Charlie Avila

All rights reserved. No part of this book may be reproduced or transmitted in any form or by any means, electronic or mechanical, including photocopying, recording, or by any information storage and retrieval system, without permission in writing from the author.

ISBN-10: **1986921298**
ISBN-13: **978-1986921299**

Printed in the United States

CONTENTS

Preface

1 The Homosexual Christian?   1

2 Sodom and Gomorrah   25

3 Standing Alone Against Homosexuality   49

4 Vile Passions – Lesbians & Homosexuals   67

5 Paul on Homosexuality   95

6 A Christian Manifesto on Homosexuality   121

Selected Bibliography   145

Scriptural Reference Index   149

PREFACE

The chapters in this book were written over several years to challenge compromising and vacillating Christians with the truths of the Bible regarding homosexuality and lesbianism. The sexual ethic presented by the LGBTQ community is corrupt, defiling and deceitful. Without fear, many people are crossing into areas of sexuality and marriage that have already received the judgment of God.

The simple contention of this book is that love without truth is no truth at all. We become enablers. The Christians who really love the homosexuals and lesbians are the ones who speak the "truth in love." If we pat these people on the back and tell them that their lifestyle is acceptable to God, then they will die in their sins and we will have blood on our hands. Sexual immorality of any type lands people in the lake of fire. Homosexuality is an eternal issue. Those who practice it will never inherit the Kingdom of God.

Our nation – as well as many nations of the world – is awash in sexual darkness, debauchery, and perversion. As a culture, we are being defiled and destroyed. Human trafficking, pornography, prostitution, adultery, unwed teen pregnancies, and sexual harassment are just some of the depraved things leading us into moral bankruptcy. Dr. Larry Nassar has abused more than 265 young girls. Ashley Madison, with 85% male subscribers, has over forty-six million users. This Canadian on-line adultery company has the motto – "Life is short. Have an affair." You can have secret adulterous affairs with other married people. Over a fifty-year period, 3,000 to 4,000 Catholic priests sexually abused tens of thousands of children and teenagers. The American comedian, Bill Cosby, has raped, sexually assaulted, and sexual abused nearly sixty women over a forty-three-year period. His preferred cowardly routine was to drug them first. Hollywood executives, movie stars, sports figures, government officials, news anchors and Christian ministers have been accused, tried, and convicted of sexual exploitation. The sexual monsters among us are famous and in positions of power and authority.

In the first chapter of this book, we answer disturbing questions presented by the proponents of "Pro-Gay Theology." Is it acceptable in the eyes of the Lord for a man to be a practicing homosexual and a practicing Christian at the same time? Were David and Jonathan homosexual lovers? Is it good for Christian denominations to ordain homosexual and lesbian bishops and pastors? Are homosexuals born gay? Is there a "gay-gene?" Did Jesus endorse homosexuality since He said nothing against it?

In the next chapter, we examine all the references in the Bible regarding "Sodom and Gomorrah." What was going on sexually in those cities? What did Jesus, the prophets, the apostles, and Moses say about "Sodom and Gomorrah?" Why did God destroy them with "fire and brimstone?"

In *Standing Alone Against Homosexuality*, we look carefully at many of the leading evangelical Pastors and churches that have embraced homosexuality. Why is there a Gay-Christian Network (GCN)? Why are Christians calling "evil good and good evil?" Should we accept the conclusions of the book *God and the Gay Christian?* Why is the prophet Micaiah such a powerful example of standing alone against what is ungodly?

In the fourth chapter, you'll find a detailed verse by verse study of Romans 1:18-28. Here we find the "lesbian verse" and why "men are burning in lust after other men." In this chapter, Paul lays out for us the root causes of homosexuality and lesbianism. The unprecedented rise of homosexuality in our day is because of the unprecedented rise of the rejection of God. When we reject God, He abandons us.

There was only one writer in the New Testament that wrote specifically about homosexuality. That writer was the apostle Paul. In *Paul on Homosexuality*, we examine the three verses that the apostle taught on homosexuality. Great practical insights come as we see what Paul wrote on this subject.

Finally, I wrote *A Christian Manifesto on Homosexuality*. This is a "position paper" from the Scriptures on how Christians should view marriage and homosexuality. We categorically reject the *"God Hates Fags"* movement. The only one who can transform a homosexual is the only one who can transform *anyone* – Jesus Christ. A personal encounter and relationship with Jesus is the only answer to homosexuality and any human need.

Jesus Christ is Lord. To God be the glory.
Charlie Avila, May 2018

1

The Homosexual Christian?

> *"But from the beginning of the creation, God 'made them male and female.' For this reason, a man shall leave his father and mother and be joined to his wife, and the two shall become one flesh; so then they are no longer two, but one flesh."* (Mark 10:6-8)

Is it acceptable in the eyes of the Lord for a man to be a practicing homosexual and a practicing Christian at the same time? Does the God of the Bible approve and welcome such a lifestyle? Were King David and Jonathan homosexual lovers? Are the strong statements against homosexuality in Leviticus really speaking about something else? Is the Lord gratified and pleased with the ordination of homosexual or lesbian Pastors, Bishops, or Priests? Is a man born gay? Does God make or create people gay? Did Jesus ever address the issue of homosexuality? I will seek to provide answers to these and other provocative questions in this study.

In this teaching, I will be using the term, "Pro-Gay Theology." What do I mean when I use this term? Joe Dallas, in his excellent book, *Desires in Conflict,* gives a clear definition:

"Pro-gay theology meets every Bible verse referring to homosexuality head-on and attempts to explain why each verse is misunderstood today. It is a bold, rapidly growing revision of the Bible which many Christians find difficult to refute. These arguments take what is obvious and claim to have discovered a different, heretofore hidden meaning. It takes scriptures we are all familiar with, gives them an entirely new interpretation, backs its claims with well-credentialed scholars, and gives birth to a new sexual ethic."[1] How are Christians, especially Pastors and other ministers of the gospel, to answer this new theology?

We must also ask ourselves these questions: How can biblical instruction that is so plain, obvious, and straightforward, be twisted around until it means the exact opposite of what God said or intended? How can a behavior that is so clearly unacceptable in God's eyes, suddenly turn out to be entirely acceptable to Him? How can people who call themselves Christians and appeal to the Bible as their final authority on life and godliness, take what is so unnatural and unhealthy, and make it appear good and wholesome? These are disturbing questions and trends. These questions must be answered. Christian believers must be thoroughly equipped in these last days to stand against such delusions and beliefs.

Were David and Jonathan Homosexuals?

Pro-Gay Theology says that King David and Jonathan were homosexual lovers based primarily on 2 Samuel 1:26.
After getting the dreadful news from an Amalekite that King Saul and his son, Jonathan, had been killed by the Philistines at Mount Gilboa, David is deeply grieved.[2] He writes a lament[3] about the death of these two Israelite leaders. You can almost hear David crying and wailing with these words – "The beauty of Israel is slain on your high places! How the mighty have fallen! O daughters of Israel, weep over Saul. How the mighty have fallen

---

[1] *Desires in Conflict*, Joe Dallas, Harvest House Publishers, Eugene, Oregon, pages 209-210.
[2] See 2 Samuel 1:1-16.
[3] A lament is a song or poem of mourning that expresses grief and sorrow.

Chapter 1: *The Homosexual Christian?*

in the midst of the battle! Jonathan was slain in your high places."[4] David is overwhelmed that his best friend is now dead. At the end of his lament, David says something about Jonathan that "Christian" homosexuals have used to justify their behavior. 2 Samuel 1:26 reads, "I am distressed for you, my brother Jonathan; you have been very pleasant (dear) to me; your love to me was wonderful, surpassing the love of women." How is a Christian to respond to such an interpretation? Were King David and Jonathan really homosexual lovers? Is this a definite biblical example of homosexuality that is accepted before God?

The answer to this question is obviously, "No." First of all, David was a man who married many wives and fathered many children. Even the names of his wives and children are clearly listed in the Bible in several places. His wives were Ahinoam, Abigail, Maacah, Haggith, Abital, Eglah, Michal, and later, Bathsheba. His sons born in Hebron were Amnon, Chileab, Absalom, Adonijah, Shephatiah, and Ithream. His sons born in Jerusalem were Shimea, Shobab, Nathan, Solomon, Ibhar, Elishama, Eliphelet, Nogah, Nepheg, and Japhia. There was also a daughter named Tamar.[5] Furthermore, *if* David was a man consumed with lust for other men, why did he have an affair with Bathsheba, Uriah's wife? Wouldn't you expect to see some kind of sexual encounter with another man? No such thing is found in the Bible. Mike Haley, a former homosexual, hits the mark: "We are, after all, talking about David – a man whose Achilles heel was his desire and insatiable lust for women. Remember, he's the same guy who had numerous concubines and wives and still couldn't be fulfilled, so he took another man's wife – Bathsheba – and killed her husband to cover his transgression. That doesn't sound much like most gay men I've met."[6]

---

[4] See 2 Samuel 1:19, 24-25.
[5] For a list of David's wives and sons see 2 Samuel 3:2-5 and 1 Chronicles 3:1-9.
[6] *101 Frequently Asked Questions About Homosexuality*, Mike Haley, Harvest House Publishers, Eugene, Oregon, pages 153-154.

Second, while Jonathan's wife is never mentioned, we do know that he had a well-known son who was lame in both feet. His name was Mephibosheth.[7] The Bible clearly reveals how much Jonathan loved David. Notice the language in these three passages: "The soul of Jonathan was knit to the soul of David, and Jonathan loved him as his own soul," "Jonathan and David made a covenant, because he loved him as his own soul," and "Jonathan again caused David to vow, because he loved him; for he loved him as he loved his own soul."[8] Isn't one of the great commandments in the Bible to "love your neighbor *as yourself?*" These men did love each other, but their relationship in the Scriptures was a simple expression of a normal, healthy

relationship between two godly men who loved and cared deeply for each other. *Nowhere do you see them moving in together. Nowhere do you see them having sex together.* Moreover, we see exactly why they made a vow and covenant together. *They were making an agreement to defend, protect, and look after each other.* Jonathan gave David his armor, sword, bow, and military belt. Jonathan told David he would test his father to see if he was still angry at him. If he was, Jonathan would give David a warning through the shooting of arrows to flee. In modern vernacular, you might say they were looking out "for each other's back." Jonathan risked his life against his own father to spare David's life. "Saul's anger was aroused against Jonathan...then Saul cast a spear at him to kill him, by which Jonathan knew that it was determined by his father to kill David."[9] *David could cry out that Jonathan's love was greater than women, because no woman had ever risked her life to save him.*[10] Jonathan jeopardized everything to deliver his best friend.

---

[7] See 2 Samuel 4:4 and 9:1-7. He was also probably called "Merib-baal" in 1 Chronicles 8:34 and 9:40.

[8] See 1 Samuel 18:1, 3, and 20:17.

[9] See 1 Samuel 20:30, 33.

[10] Actually, Michal, Saul's daughter, did help David escape from Saul, but she was never threatened with death for aiding him. See 1 Samuel 19:11-18.

Chapter 1: *The Homosexual Christian?*

Third, anyone who reads the story of Jonathan and David in 1 Samuel, Chapters 13-31, with honesty and integrity, knows that Jonathan and David actually spent very little time together. In 1 Samuel 14, when Jonathan attacks the garrison of the Philistines, David is never mentioned. In 1 Samuel 17, when David defeated Goliath, Jonathan is not found. In fact, in all of David's wanderings as he is fleeing from Saul and all his enemies in 1 Samuel, Chapters 21-30, Jonathan only sees David one time. In 1 Samuel 23:16-18, David is with 600 other men in the wilderness of Ziph, and Jonathan goes out, as any good friend would do, and he "strengthens his hand in God." In verse 18, we are told immediately that "David stayed in the woods, and Jonathan went to his own house." They didn't have a sexual encounter in the wilderness with 600 other men watching. After a brief time of encouragement, both men went their separate ways. And when Jonathan was killed on Mount Gilboa along with his father, David was down in the southern town of Ziklag.[11] *So you don't find anywhere in the Bible where David and Jonathan lived together as homosexual lovers.*

Why don't gay theologians quote these verses: "Now Saul's daughter Michal was in love with David, and when they told Saul about it, he was pleased. Then Saul gave him his daughter Michal in marriage. Saul realized that the LORD was with David and that his daughter Michal loved David."[12] David is never given in marriage to Jonathan. We don't see a "gay wedding." Here we have another wife of David's who really loves him and actually marries him. Later on, in 1 Samuel 19, we even read of their marriage bed because Michal places an idol with some goat's hair to make it look like David is sick and in bed under the covers. Nowhere in the Scriptures do we see any mention of David's and Jonathan's bed where they make love.

Why don't gay theologians quote 1 Kings 5:1: "Now Hiram king of Tyre sent his servants to Solomon, because he heard that they had anointed him king in place of his father, *for Hiram had always loved David.*" The United Bible Societies (UBS) translation notes on 2 Samuel 1:26 make this interesting

---

[11] See 1 Samuel, Chapters 30 and 31.
[12] See 1 Samuel 18:20, 27-28.

observation – "The idea of love between two political figures is not uncommon in the Old Testament. Non-biblical texts from the ancient Near East show that kings who were in political alliance were said to 'love' one another. In such contexts, the primary semantic element is that of loyalty. Hiram is said to have 'loved' David, and the context clearly shows the political overtones of the word." Certainly, anyone who truly understands the relationship between David and Jonathan can speak of their loyalty to one another.

Also, when you look at David's and Jonathan's parents – Jesse and Saul – both of these men were married and fathered many children. Jesse had eight sons and two daughters.[13] Saul was married to Ahinoam and fathered six children – (four sons) Jonathan, Malchishua, Abinadab, Esh-baal and (two daughters) Merab and Michal.[14] Saul even had a concubine named Rizpah through whom he fathered two more sons.[15] My point is that there is no history of homosexuality in David's or Jonathan's family line.

The simple conclusion is that David and Jonathan were good friends that genuinely loved each other. They were not homosexual lovers. Both men were married and had children. They were never involved together in homosexual activity.

Is the Abomination of Leviticus Idolatry Only?

Pro-Gay Theology says that practices found in Leviticus 18 and 20 that are called an abomination are actually condemning idolatry, not homosexuality. Thus, if homosexuality is practiced apart from idolatry, then it must be acceptable or permissible by God.

Leviticus 18 gives you God's laws and views on various sexual sins. It's filled with a bunch of "you shall not's." Leviticus 20 provides the punishment for such sins. It says to "put people to death," "cut them off from My people," and even, "burn them in the fire!" Let's look at two verses in Leviticus because

---

[13] See 1 Samuel 16:5-10, 17:12, and 1 Chronicles 2:13-16.
[14] See 1 Samuel 31:2, 1 Chronicles 8:33, 9:39, and 10:2.
[15] See 2 Samuel 3:7 and 21:8, 11.

Chapter 1: *The Homosexual Christian?*

they give you the clearest denunciation of homosexuality found anywhere in the Bible.

Leviticus 18:22 reads, "You shall not lie with a male as with a woman. It is an abomination." Here's how this verse appears in various translations:

- "No man is to have sexual relations with another man; God hates that." (TEV)
- "Do not practice homosexuality, having sex with another man as with a woman. It is a detestable sin." (NLT)
- "It is disgusting for a man to have sex with another man." (CEV)
- "Men, you must not have sexual relations with another man as with a woman. That is a terrible sin!" (ERV)

I don't mean to be cynical, but you don't need to be a Hebrew scholar to understand these verses. These verses *clearly* teach that homosexuality – sex between two men – is something God hates. It is detestable. It is an abomination.

First of all, let's define this word using a standard dictionary. Abomination (noun) = "A feeling of utter hostility and disgust; revulsion, abhorrence, anathema, detestation, hate, hatred, horror, loathing, repugnance, repulsion; an object of extreme dislike." Basically, an abomination is anything that God hates intensely. It's the strongest word in the English language for hatred.

The problem for the gay "Christian" community doesn't seem to be the *definition* of the word "abomination." It's the *application* of this word. Their simple claim is that the homosexuality of Leviticus 18 and 20 was practiced solely with idolatry. It is true that idolatry, graven images or sacrifices to false gods are called "abominations" in the Bible:
- Idolatry/Idols – Deuteronomy 13:13-14, 17:3-4, 32:16, 1 Kings 21:26, 2 Kings 21:11-12, Jeremiah 16:18, Ezekiel 6:9, 7, 8, 14:6, 16:36, 23:36-37, and Malachi 2:11.
- Graven, carved images (and their worship) – Deuteronomy 7:25-26, 27:15, and 2 Kings 23:13.

- Sacrifice of children to false gods – Deuteronomy 12:31, 2 Kings 16:3, 2 Chronicles 28:3, Jeremiah 32:35, 44:3-5, Ezekiel 16:36.

But notice all these other sins in the Bible that are called abominations:
- Bestiality – Leviticus 18:23 and 18:26
- Offering a blemished animal to the Lord – Deuteronomy 17:1
- Sorcery, witchcraft, and divination – Deuteronomy 18:9-12
- Men wearing women's clothes, women wearing men's clothes – Deuteronomy 22:5
- Offering the wages of a prostitute or price of a dog – Deuteronomy 23:18, Proverbs 15:8 and 21:27
- Marrying your 1st wife a 2nd time, after she was married to another man – Deuteronomy 24:4; Jeremiah 3:1
- Differing weights and measures (cheating) – Deuteronomy 25:14-16, Proverbs 11:1, 20:16 and 20:23
- A perverse or unjust man – Proverbs 3:32, 11:20 and 29:27
- A bloodthirsty and deceitful man – Psalms 5:6
- Wickedness – Proverbs 8:7, 15:8-9, 15:26, and 21:27
- Lying – Proverbs 12:22
- The proud in heart – Proverbs 16:5, Ezekiel 16:50
- Justifying the wicked; condemning the innocent – Proverbs 17:15
- Turning away from listening to God's Word – Proverbs 28:9
- Worship from a wicked heart (doing evil) – Isaiah 1:12-16
- Adultery – Ezekiel 22:11

There is even a list of seven abominations in Proverbs 6:16-19 – 1) A proud look, 2) A lying tongue, 3) Hands that shed innocent blood, 4) A heart that devises wicked plans, 5) Feet that are swift in running to evil, 6) A false witness who speaks lies and 7) And one who sows discord (dissension) among brethren.

Thus, idolatry is not exclusively associated with "abomination." There are many different abominations in the Bible.

But beyond these spiritual exercises seeking to find a proper definition and application of "abomination," let's look at Leviticus 18:22 itself. "You shall not lie with a male as with a woman. It is an abomination." There is no mention in this verse about idolatry. There is nothing about this act taking place in some kind of pagan or idolatrous worship service. This verse is easy, simple, and understandable. *God's people were not to practice homosexuality.* Men were not to have sex with other men as they do with women. God hates that. It is abominable.

As you look at the whole of Leviticus, Chapter 18, there are other sexual sins that are forbidden – incest, adultery, fornication, bestiality, or sex with any relatives. These sins "defile" individuals (v24) and they "defile" the land (v25). The strong conclusion at verses 27-29 is "for all of these abominations the men of the land have done, who were before you, and thus the land is defiled, lest the land vomit you out also when you defile it, as it vomited out the nations that were before you. For whoever commits any of these abominations, the persons who commit them shall be cut off from among their people." What words! "Abomination," "defiled," "vomit," "vomited," "abominations," and "cut off."

Let's look at the second verse, Leviticus 20:13: "If a man lies with a male as he lies with a woman, both of them have committed an abomination. They shall surely be put to death. Their blood shall be upon them." The NLT says, "If a man practices homosexuality, having sex with another man as with a woman, both men have committed a detestable act. They must both be put to death, for they are guilty of a capital offense." Again, there is no mistaking the language here. However, this verse goes a step beyond Leviticus 18:22. It again says that homosexuality is an abomination, but now it gives the punishment for such a sin under the Mosaic law – "They shall surely be put to death. Their blood shall be upon them." What does it mean that "their blood shall be upon them?" Some translations read, "They are responsible for their own death" or "They have brought it on themselves." In other words, they have been warned. If they suffered death, sickness, or calamity, it's their own fault. God is saying to all people, that if anyone practices homosexuality, He is going to oppose and resist him on every side. People have been warned, and if they continue on in homosexuality, they are in willful disobedience to the clear commands of God. They themselves are responsible for the consequences.

When Paul was teaching the elders of the church at Miletus, he said, "I testify to you this day that I am innocent of the blood of all men. For I have not shunned to declare to you the whole counsel of God."[16] If Paul had withheld truth from others, and people died in their sins, then he would be held responsible for their blood. This is exactly what happened to the prophet Ezekiel. God warned him, "When I say to the wicked, 'O wicked man, you will surely die,' and you do not speak out to dissuade him from his ways, that wicked man will die for his sin, and *I will hold you accountable for his blood*. But if you do warn the wicked man to turn from his ways and he does not do so, he will die for his sin, but *you will have saved yourself*."[17] In other words, Ezekiel would clear himself of any responsibility because he warned people about their sins and the consequences. *In the case of homosexuality, everyone has been warned. God has spoken. And we must speak. Homosexuality is playing with fire, and if a gay "Christian" suffers a broken life with broken relationships and emotional turmoil, he is responsible for these troubles. His blood is on his head.*

In summary, both of these verses in Leviticus are clear, straightforward commandments from the Lord forbidding the practice of homosexuality.

Homosexual Bishops and Pastors?

Pro-Gay Theology says that it is acceptable in God's eyes to ordain homosexual Bishops and Pastors as long as they are in long-term, same-sex relationships.

---

[16] See Acts 20:27-28.
[17] See Ezekiel 33:8-9.

Chapter 1: *The Homosexual Christian?*

June 7, 2003 was a fateful day, not only for the Episcopal Diocese of New Hampshire, but also for the Episcopal Church of the United States. It was on this day that the openly gay Gene Robinson (pictured) was elected as the Ninth Bishop of New Hampshire, a position he assumed on March 7, 2004. His election set off a war in his denomination that threatened to tear apart many dioceses and churches. He was married to the former Isabella Martin for twelve years and fathered two daughters. The marriage ended in divorce, and in 1986, at the age of 39, he confessed to his bishop that he was a homosexual.  Shortly afterward, he moved in with his partner, Mark Andrew, an official with the New Hampshire Department of Health and Human Services. (It should be noted that they have recently divorced.)

How does Bishop Robinson justify his lifestyle? In a 2003 interview on *60 Minutes*, he tells CBS correspondent Ed Bradley: "As an openly gay man, I'm not way out there. I'm not something odd and unusual. I think I'm probably dangerous because I'm pretty mainstream. I've got a mainstream family. I believe in the church. I believe in God, and I'm only dangerous because I'm not weird." According to the interview, "He believes God is doing something new – leading the Church and society to a greater acceptance of homosexuals. 'I think God is meaning for gay and lesbian folk to have a full, whole, and complete life – both as citizens of this country and as members of the church.'" These words are very telling – *He believes God is doing something new.* The "something new" is that homosexuality is *now* acceptable in God's sight.

Not everyone was buying into this new thinking. A few days after Robinson's consecration as Bishop, Father Don Wilson, a man who had served faithfully as an Episcopalian Pastor for nearly 50 years, was fired for refusing to recognize the bishop's authority. When asked by Ed Bradley why he can't accept the bishop's authority, even though he's sworn an oath to do so, Wilson responds, "I've never been in trouble before. That's strange isn't it, because the first part of my oath was the authority of Scripture. The second part of the oath was to teach it. And the third part of the oath was to protect the people from strange and erroneous doctrines. Then way down the list it says, 'Be subject to the bishops, their godly judgments and godly admonitions.' And I didn't find any in him." What a word! What is Father Wilson's advice to Bible-believing Christians? "Stand. Just don't accept it. Take a stand against it. Do not cooperate with it. Do not support it. Do not recognize it."

Lisa Bell, a member of one of the churches under Robinson's jurisdiction, makes these insightful comments: "It has to do with him living an immoral lifestyle and being a leader. I don't expect the chief of police to be a bank robber. I don't expect the chief of the fire department to be an arsonist. If he's going to hold a higher office, he's going to be held to a higher moral standard. He's the head of a church, for God's sake."[18]

Does the Bible say anything about the position of a bishop and its qualifications? 1 Timothy 3:1-2 starts out – "This is a faithful saying: If a man desires the position of a bishop, he desires a good work. A bishop then must be blameless, the husband of one wife." Paul then adds in verses 4-5, the bishop must be "one who rules his own house well, having his children in submission with all reverence, for if a man does not know how to rule his own house, how will he take care of the church of God?" Titus 1:6, 9 reads that a bishop must be "blameless, the husband of one wife, having faithful children not accused of dissipation or insubordination. For a bishop must be blameless…holding fast the faithful word as he has been taught, that he may be able, by sound doctrine, both to exhort and convict those who contradict." Even deacons have similar qualifications: "Let deacons be the husbands of one wife, ruling their children and their own houses well."[19] Among many important requirements, the Bible tells us here that bishops must be "blameless," "the husband of one wife," and have "children" who are serving the Lord. Furthermore, even the priests of the Old Testament were given these instructions – "They must not marry women defiled by prostitution or divorced

---

[18] Biographical information on Gene Robinson was taken directly from the Episcopal Diocese of New Hampshire website at www.nhepiscopal.org. The Ed Bradley interview was transcribed and available at www.cbsnews.com.
[19] See 1 Timothy 3:12.

Chapter 1: *The Homosexual Christian?*

from their husbands, because priests are holy to their God. He must not marry a widow, a divorced woman, or a woman defiled by prostitution, but only a virgin from his own people, so he will not defile (profane) his offspring among his people. I am the LORD, who makes him holy."[20] The priest had to marry a virgin woman. Even from the women he could not marry, they were still all women. *The truth is that there is not a single reference in the entire Bible of a homosexual who was ordained and consecrated as a minister for the Lord.* Apart from the notable exception of the apostle Paul, who remained single his entire life, all of God's priests, prophets, apostles, pastors, teachers, and evangelists were men who married women and fathered children. Again, *there is no minister in the Bible who was a homosexual.*

Consider this: Adam was married to Eve; Noah was married to his wife and fathered three sons; Abraham was married to Sarah; Isaac to Rebekah; Jacob to Rachel and Leah; Esau to Mahalath and other wives; Joseph to Asenath; Moses to Zipporah; Aaron to Elisheba; Gideon had many wives and seventy sons; Samson had a Philistine wife and Delilah; Boaz married Ruth; Elkanah had Hannah; Samuel had a wife and two sons; Saul to Ahinoam; both David and Solomon had many wives; Uriah to Bathsheba; and all the kings of Judah and Israel married, usually multiple wives, and fathered children. Job was married to his wife; Esther was married to King Xerxes; Isaiah to the prophetess; Hosea to Gomer; Zechariah to Elizabeth; Joseph with Mary; Peter to his wife; Philip the evangelist and his wife had four daughters; and Aquila to Priscilla. Even for those men with no mention of a wife – Joshua, Elijah, Elisha, John the Baptist, or Daniel – we know they were godly men who would have surely rejected homosexuality. *If there are so many gay ministers now, how come there were none then? We have no examples because there are no examples.* We have homosexual bishops today because corrupt men and women have chosen to appoint them according to their lust and vile passions.

The floodgates are beginning to open in certain denominations. The Evangelical Lutheran Church of America (ELCA) recently welcomed back seven homosexual ministers

---

[20] See Leviticus 21:7, 15-16.

who had been barred. This is now the largest denomination in the U.S. to allow homosexual ministers. Other denominations that ordain homosexuals include the U.S. Episcopal Church, United Church of Christ, and the Presbyterian Church (U.S.A.).

Are Gay People Born that Way? Did God Make Me Gay?

Pro-Gay Theology says that certain people are "born gay." In other words, God made them that way. They are born with "gay genetics" or they have the "gay gene."

Let's get right to the point: First, there are no verses in the Bible that teach that God makes or creates anyone with a homosexual orientation. And obviously, there is no mention in the Scriptures of a "gay gene" or "gay genetics." No one in the Bible was "born a homosexual." Homosexuality is not the result of creation, but the result of the Fall.[21] Second, there has *never* been any scientific (bias or unbiased) study that has proved that anyone is "born gay."

Let's look at four "sources"[22] that are often quoted (or misquoted) by homosexuals, both "Christian" and non-Christian, to say that people are "born gay" or have a "gay gene." In no particular order:

<u>Dr. Dean Hamer and the X Chromosome</u>: First, Hamer is a homosexual who lives with his "life partner," Joe Wilson. Second, he is a graduate of Harvard Medical School and is a researcher at the National Cancer Institute. When his study was released in 1993, it created a media storm, and *Time* magazine published a sensational (and deceptive) cover story – *Born Gay: Science*[23] *Finds a Genetic Link*. Pro-gay believers need to know right up front that no one has ever replicated his results. He

---

[21] It is not an issue of nature, but of nurture. Homosexuality did not come because of Genesis 1-2, but Genesis 3.

[22] Numerous books, articles, and chapters have been written discussing these studies. I do not plan to give all the details, but I will summarize and condense the main points that are relevant to the discussion.

[23] Note the wording – "Science," not Dr. Hamer, a homosexual, had found the genetic link for homosexuality. One man's erroneous research does not equal all of "Science," especially since no other researcher has ever come up with the same results in *any* study.

Chapter 1: *The Homosexual Christian?*

claimed that after studying forty pairs of gay (non-identical) brothers, 33 pairs, or 83%, had the same five (X-linked) genetic markers, thus indicating a genetic cause for homosexuality.

We know his results are false for several reasons. First, most of the general population has the identical gene sequence as these homosexual pairs. In other words, it's nothing out of the ordinary. As further proof, some of these same heterosexual brothers of the 33 pairs also had the same gene sequence. Second, the seven homosexual pairs that didn't work for Hamer did not have the gene sequence at all. Finally, and most damaging of all, even Hamer in the end had to report that "we never found a single family in which homosexuality was distributed in the obvious sort of pattern."[24]

Dr. Simon LeVay and the Hypothalamus: Once again, it's important to note that Dr. LeVay (pictured) is openly homosexual. After the death of his homosexual lover, he was determined to find a "genetic cause for homosexuality." His research is clearly biased because he himself admitted that he set out to affect legal and religious attitudes toward homosexuality. By all medical standards, he is a brilliant neuroscientist, having taught at such prestigious institutions such as Harvard  Medical School, the Salk Institute, Stanford University, and the University of California at San Diego.

In 1991, he released a study based on the cadavers of six women, nineteen homosexuals, and sixteen heterosexual men where he examined a portion of the hypothalamus (INAH-3). He found that the hypothalamus of the nineteen gay men was twice as small as that of the heterosexual men, and basically the same size as the six women. His erroneous conclusion was that perhaps homosexual men have a "sexual orientation" like that of women. First, his findings, like Hamer's above, have never been duplicated by any researcher, scientist, or medical group. Second, and probably his most glaring error, all of the nineteen men tested had died of AIDS complications. Some researchers claim that the

---

[24] *The Science of Desire*, Dean Hamer and Peter Copeland, Simon and Schuster, New York, NY, page 104.

size difference in the hypothalamus may have been the result of their disease not their sexuality. Third, and this is my personal observation, how can you draw any important conclusions based on a total of 41 cadavers? You're not going to sell "conclusive research" on such a small sampling. Furthermore, LeVay never proved or knew that the sixteen men were all heterosexual. He assumed they were but he wasn't sure. Finally, notice this point, as in all the studies, *Dr. LeVay himself admits that he didn't find the "gay gene."* In his own words, from his own book: "It's important to stress what I didn't find. I did not prove that homosexuality is genetic or find a genetic cause for being gay. I didn't show that gay men are born that way, the most common mistake people make in interpreting my work. Nor did I locate a gay center in the brain."[25] Gay "Christians" cannot use either Hamer's or LeVay's research to "prove" homosexuality is genetic in origin.

Michael Bailey and Richard Pillard Twin Studies: Again, Psychiatrist Pillard is openly homosexual, and Bailey, a psychologist, is a gay rights advocate at Northwestern University. They conducted studies using identical twins, non-identical twins, non-twins, and adoptive brothers where at least one of the pairs was a homosexual. I will not report on the non-twins and adoptive brothers because they were insignificant to the overall results.

Here's what they found – that 52% of the identical twins were both homosexual, but only 22 of the non-identical twins were both homosexual. Thus, Bailey and Pillard concluded, that the higher percentages of shared homosexuality among the identical twins proved that the root cause of homosexuality was genetic.

Again, no one has come up with the same results. Again, we have homosexual or pro-homosexual researchers. Here is a simple answer to disprove this study – identical twins have identical genes. This would mean that we should see 100% homosexuality, not 52%, if it's all tied to genes. This is not what they found. Thus, genetics alone cannot account for the 48% that were not homosexual. In March of 1992, the *British Journal of Psychiatry* published a report of a very similar study that found

---

[25] *The Sexual Brain*, Simon LeVay, MIT Press, Cambridge, MA, page 122.

Chapter 1: *The Homosexual Christian?*

only 20% of the homosexual twins had a homosexual co-twin.[26] So a similar study produced vastly different results.

<u>Alfred Kinsey and the Kinsey Reports</u>: Dr. Kinsey, an American biologist, graduated from Harvard University. He passed away in 1956. It is probably not commonly known that his parents were very devout Christian believers and brought him up in the ways of the Lord. He founded what is now called the Kinsey Institute for Research on Sex, Gender, and Reproduction at Indiana University where he was a professor. His now-famous *Kinsey Reports* actually had nothing to do with finding a "gay gene" or linking homosexuality to genetics. Probably the most important piece of totally erroneous information from his studies was his "report" that 10%[27] of the population was homosexual.

Why do I bring up this report? Because it gets thrown around by uninformed people who are so desperate to find some scientific study that will support their homosexual lifestyle. Kinsey said nothing about "gay genes" or "gay genetics." People regularly quote the "Kinsey Reports" as their "proof" that homosexuality is linked to genetics. This is completely false.

What does the Bible say about how we are created? The most famous verse is Genesis 1:27, "So God created man in His own image; in the image of God He created him; male and female He created them." You are not created "gay." You are created in the image of God. Notice the words – *"male and female"* He created them. Now notice what the very next verse says, "Then God blessed them, and God said to them, 'Be fruitful and multiply; fill the earth and subdue it.'" How can you populate this planet or "fill the earth?" The only way to be fruitful and multiply is for men and women to marry, have sexual relations, and produce more children. Homosexuals and lesbians cannot do this. It is unnatural – against nature. When the Lord started talking about the "marriage covenant" and a "man and the wife of his youth," and why He "hated divorce," He spoke through Malachi the prophet saying that the reason He joined them together as "one

---

[26] See Dallas' information in *Desires in Conflict*, page 205.
[27] The actual number for females is just above 1% and about 2% for males. See the National Health and Social Life Survey.

flesh and one spirit" was because He wanted "godly offspring."[28] Again, this cannot be produced in a homosexual relationship.

In Genesis 5:1-2, we have similar words as Genesis 1:27: "In the day that God created man, He made him in the likeness of God. He created them male and female, and blessed them." Jesus quotes this truth in Matthew 19:4, "And He answered and said to them, 'Have you not read that He who made them at the beginning made them male and female.'" And again, in Mark 10:6, "But from the beginning of the creation, God made them male and female." James 3:9 says that "men have been made in God's likeness." Here's a very important verse: "For a man indeed ought not to cover his head, since he is the image and glory of God; but woman is the glory of man. For man is not from woman, but woman from man. Nor was man created for the woman, but woman for the man."[29] This is a powerful declaration that all Bible-believing Christians must make with truth and conviction – *"The woman was created for the man."* Women are not created for other women nor men for men. Man was created in the image of God and for the glory of God. We were not created for another man or multiple men. This is confusion.

Jesus Said Nothing About or Against Homosexuality?

Pro-Gay Theology says that Jesus said nothing about homosexuality. Therefore, if He didn't say anything against it, it must be acceptable to Him.

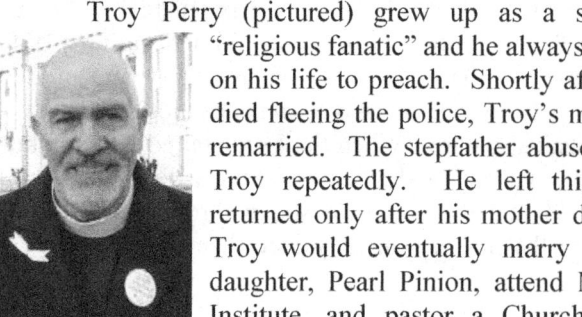

Troy Perry (pictured) grew up as a self-described "religious fanatic" and he always sensed a call on his life to preach. Shortly after his father died fleeing the police, Troy's mother, Edith, remarried. The stepfather abused the young Troy repeatedly. He left this home and returned only after his mother divorced him. Troy would eventually marry a preacher's daughter, Pearl Pinion, attend Moody Bible Institute, and pastor a Church of God in

---

[28] See Malachi 2:14-16.
[29] See 1 Corinthians 11:7-9.

Illinois. While married, he began to have multiple sexual affairs with other men and, at a very young age, he was forced to resign as Pastor and leave town immediately. He moved to Southern California and became the Pastor of a Church of God in Prophecy. His wife found a copy of the book, *The Homosexual in America*, under his mattress and his marriage soon ended in divorce. On October 6, 1968, Troy Perry started a new church, Metropolitan Community Church (MCC). This new church and movement would welcome gay, lesbian, bisexual, and transsexual "Christians." This denomination now has over 300 congregations in 18 countries at the time of this writing. His autobiography, *The Lord is My Shepherd and He Knows I'm Gay*, along with other books on gay issues, seeks to promote the homosexual lifestyle as something completely acceptable in God's eyes.

Joe Dallas writes, "Troy Perry makes much of his arguments based on silence (as most gay Christian leaders do): Perry says, 'As for the question, what did Jesus say about homosexuality? The answer is simple. Jesus said nothing. Not one thing. Nothing! Jesus was more interested in love.'"[30] He says repeatedly, "I always say that as a Christian I cannot find any passage in the Gospels in which Jesus condemned homosexuality." How are we to respond to such a statement?

First, it is true, you will not find the word "homosexual" in any of the four gospels. It's also true that Jesus did not specifically condemn homosexuality. But Jesus did affirm the biblical model and norm for sexuality in marriage relationships. Mark 10:6-8 reads, "From the beginning of the creation, God 'made them male and female. For this reason, a man shall leave his father and mother and be joined to his wife, and the two shall become one flesh;' so then they are no longer two, but one flesh."[31] Notice that Jesus went all the way back to the creation account in Genesis, Chapters 1-2, to reinforce God's original intent for marriage. It was not divorce or homosexuality. It was

---

[30] *Desires in Conflict*, page 218.
[31] It is amazing that when the general assembly of the ELCA denomination met to vote on whether Jesus' words in this very passage should be the accepted biblical standard for marriage relationships, the "no" votes outnumbered the "yes" votes. This paved the way to reinstate defrocked homosexual ministers.

"male" and "female" coming together as "man" and "wife." It was a "man" leaving his "father" and "mother" so that he could be joined with his "wife" and they could be "one flesh." The words here in Mark are repeated almost word for word in Matthew 19:4-6. Even when Jesus spoke against divorce, it was always in the context of "husband" and "wife," or "man" and "woman." For example, Luke 16:18, "Whoever divorces his *wife* and marries another commits adultery; and whoever marries *her* who is divorced from *her husband* commits adultery."

Second, this argument of pro-gay theology is fundamentally an argument from silence. They believe that since Jesus said nothing for or against homosexuality, therefore, it must be okay. But here is a critical point for me – Then why is Jesus, the Lamb of God, going to marry His "wife," called the "bride," "the Lamb's wife" at His "marriage" at the end of the age? Revelation 19:7-8 reads, "Let us be glad and rejoice and give Him glory, for the marriage of the Lamb has come, and His wife has made herself ready. And to her it was granted to be arrayed in fine linen, clean and bright, for the fine linen is the righteous acts of the saints." When the time comes for the Lord to get married, He marries a woman! Of course, this "woman" is the redeemed of the Lord – those who are genuinely saved. Is He not putting His stamp of approval, forever, on marriage between a husband and wife? In Revelation 21:2, the apostle John "saw the holy city, New Jerusalem, coming down out of heaven from God, prepared as a bride adorned for her husband." A few verses later, at verse 9, an angel tells him, "Come, I will show you the bride, the Lamb's wife."

Going further still, when the apostle Paul wanted to establish the husband and wife relationship in marriage as God's standard, and teach us about married life, he wrote in Ephesians 5:25, "Husbands, love your wives, just as Christ also loved the church and gave Himself for her." While he's talking about husband (man) and wife (woman) relationships, he's really "speaking concerning Christ and the church" (Ephesians 5:32). The body of Christ is the bride of Christ. In verse 30, Paul says that the true Christian believers "are members of His body." Speaking to believers again, in 2 Corinthians 11:2, he says, "For I am jealous for you with godly jealousy. For I have betrothed you

Chapter 1: *The Homosexual Christian?*

to one husband, that I may present you as a chaste virgin to Christ." Jesus will not marry another "man." He marries His bride. She is a "chaste virgin," who is "pure and spotless, a glorious church" because He gave Himself "for her."

Why does Jesus not mention or condemn homosexuality in the gospels? Because everything around Him was "man" and "woman," "male" and "female," "husband" and "wife," and "father" and "mother." Everyone – from the apostles He appointed to the parables He spoke, from the people He healed to the family He was raised in, from the teachings He gave to the Roman governor (Pilate) who ruled – were married people who were "husband" and "wife." Jesus appointed no homosexual apostles. Jesus gave no homosexual parables. Jesus was not raised in a home with homosexuals. Jesus healed no homosexuals dying of AIDS or any other diseases. *No doubt, homosexuality existed, but it wasn't around, wasn't promoted, wasn't prominent, wasn't a "vital issue," and wasn't a part of the family life in Israel!*

The truth is that Peter was married and so were the other apostles. Jesus was raised in a home where Joseph was the father and Mary was the mother. His forerunner, John the Baptist, was raised by Zechariah the husband and Elizabeth the wife. He taught us to "honor your father and your mother." He was seen as an infant by Anna who was a widow that once had a husband. He gave parables in Matthew and Luke that included a man with his wife and children, or a man married to a wife. Pilate was married. Herod had a wife and then someone else's wife! Jesus raised a young girl who was dead and returned her to her "father and mother." *Let's take up this argument from silence – Why didn't Jesus ENDORSE HOMOSEXUALITY?* If gay-theology is correct and it's okay with Jesus, why didn't He just say so! At least once, He could have mentioned honoring your "two daddies" or "two mommies." At least once, He could have given support to homosexual marriage by going to a wedding in Cana where two guys made a "life-long commitment to one another." At least once, He should have sanctioned a father with two homosexual sons, where one of them went off with his homosexual lover. *Since Jesus didn't condemn homosexuality, why didn't He endorse it? If Jesus is behind the present-day, gay Christian*

THE CHRISTIAN & HOMOSEXUALITY

movement, why not at least give us one line of Scripture saying it is okay? We already have verses in the Old and New Testament that soundly condemn the homosexual lifestyle. In the words of Jesus Himself in Luke 16:31, "If you do not hear Moses and the prophets, neither will you be persuaded" if Jesus tells you "no." We already have Moses and Paul; we don't need any further witnesses. It was Paul who quoted Moses saying, "Every matter must be established by the testimony of two or three witnesses." *The truth is we have no witness in Scripture promoting, endorsing, or accepting homosexuality.*

I really like Joe Dallas' words: "Are we really to believe that Jesus did not care about wife beating or incest just because He said nothing about them? Are not the prohibitions against incest in Leviticus and 1 Corinthians, as well as Paul's admonition to husbands to love their wives, enough to instruct in these matters without being mentioned in the Gospels? There are any number of evil behaviors that Christ did not mention by name. Surely, we don't condone them for that reason alone! Likewise, Jesus' silence on homosexuality in no way negates the very specific prohibitions against it which appear elsewhere in both Old and New Testaments."[32]

In summary, we have drawn the following conclusions in this important teaching:
- David and Jonathan were not homosexuals. They were both married and fathered numerous children. David was also "loved" by Michal (a woman) and Hiram (a male king).
- The key verses in Leviticus condemning homosexuality were not practiced along with idolatry. They were sexual sins alone as were the other sins in those same chapters like incest, adultery, fornication, and bestiality. There are many abominations in the Bible that don't include idolatry.
- The Bible clearly teaches that a bishop was to be the "husband of one wife" and have "children." There are no

---

[32] See *Desires in Conflict*, pages 219-220.

Chapter 1: *The Homosexual Christian?*

homosexual deacons, elders, apostles, prophets, priests, or any other minister found in the Bible. None.
- No verses in the Bible say that we were "born gay." No scientific study of any kind has ever proved that homosexuality is linked to genetics. You were created in the image of God. The woman was created for man, as Paul declares.
- Jesus never endorses homosexuality. He appealed to the Genesis account at creation as God's model "from the beginning." He never appointed anyone who was a homosexual as one of His apostles or followers. Everyone in Jesus' life, ministry, family, teaching, and parables were "male and female" or "husband and wife." Jesus didn't have to specifically condemn homosexuality because He didn't need to repeat what was said elsewhere.

Pro-gay theology is false, misleading, and unbiblical. It should be soundly rejected by Christian believers everywhere. The traditional beliefs, though old, are tried and true. The established, time-honored truths of marriage, sexuality, and personal relationships found in the Bible are still the foundation for life and godliness. The new morality is not a new truth, but an old lie. David and Jonathan were not homosexual lovers. Homosexuality is an abomination to God. Bishops must be the husband of one wife. We are created in the image of God. The woman was created for man. Jesus will marry His bride, the Lamb's wife, at the end of the age.

2

Sodom and Gomorrah

"In a similar way, Sodom and Gomorrah and the surrounding towns gave themselves up to sexual immorality and perversion. They serve as an example of those who suffer the punishment of eternal fire." (Jude 1:7)

On November 10, 1978, San Francisco supervisor, Dan White, resigned his position. He cited his insufficient salary of $9,600 per year and relentless opposition from the ultra-liberal mayor, George Moscone (pictured), and the openly gay supervisor, Harvey Milk, as reasons for his resignation. After some urging by conservative colleagues and friends, Supervisor White went to city hall to ask Mayor Moscone for his seat again.
Moscone was actually leaning toward restoring White, but Milk convinced the mayor otherwise.

November 27, 1978 was the fateful day. Dan White entered city hall through a first-floor window with a loaded gun and ten rounds of ammunition. This entry allowed him to avoid the newly installed metal detectors. He went to the mayor's office seeking reappointment. When the mayor refused, White shot him four times, including two shots to the head. He reloaded his gun, walked down the hall to Harvey Milk's office, and shot him five times. Both men were now dead. White later turned himself in and confessed to the murders.

The president of the Board of Supervisors, Dianne Feinstein, heard the shots, ran to Milk's office, and found him dead. Later, because of her position as Board President, she broadcast the sensational double-murders through a special television announcement. A week later, on December 4, 1978, Feinstein was sworn in as the new mayor of San Francisco. Moscone, who celebrated his 49th birthday only three days earlier, was a married man with four children. Milk, who was Jewish and a Korean War veteran, was only forty-eight. Both men eventually became icons and martyrs of the gay rights movement.

At the controversial trial, Dr. Martin Blinder, a forensic psychiatrist, testified that Dan White committed these deadly acts in a state of depression. Dr. Blinder said in court that White, who was once very health conscious, was now eating too much sugary foods and drinks like Twinkies and Coca-Cola. He argued that White could not be held responsible for first-degree murder because of his "diminished capacity." This became known as the "Twinkie Defense." The jury bought into this testimony and eventually convicted him of voluntary manslaughter. He was sentenced to seven years in prison. The rioting that resulted from this verdict became known as the "White Night Riots."

After serving five years in Soledad State Prison, White was released. Two years later, on October 21, 1985, Daniel James "Dan" White committed suicide when he placed a garden hose from the exhaust pipe to the inside of his car. The "All-American boy" was dead of carbon monoxide poisoning. The "most hated man in San Francisco history" was gone.

The deaths of Moscone and Milk became a defining moment in homosexual politics. They gave a sympathetic voice to the gay rights agenda in San Francisco and elsewhere. The momentous events of November 27th live on in the gay

Chapter 2: *Sodom & Gomorrah*

consciousness. Harvey Milk has become the poster child for gay politicians and the gay agenda in this country.

I also want to talk about another momentous event that defines much of God's agenda in the history of the world. I want to teach on Sodom and Gomorrah. What happened to these cities should give Christians an authoritative voice on the subject of homosexuality. The destruction of Sodom and Gomorrah by the judgment of God has been set forth as a historic example of how God will deal with individuals, families, communities, states, and nations that embrace homosexuality. As tragic as the events of November 27th were, they pale in comparison to the events of Genesis 19. Let's study what the Bible teaches us about Sodom and Gomorrah.

Sodom and Gomorrah in Jude

Jude 1:5-7 mentions three of God's most awesome biblical judgments. First, in verse 5, God "destroyed" His people that He "saved out of Egypt." As one commentator says, "The same Lord who saves is the same Lord who destroys."[33] "Saved, but destroyed" is the sad testimony of the wilderness generation. Second, in verse 6, God has put the "angels who sinned" (2 Peter 2:4) into "everlasting chains" to await the judgment of God. First, it's the men of earth, and then it's the angels of heaven. Third, verse 7 gives us the terrible judgment upon "Sodom and Gomorrah." This verse provides great insights into what happened on that ominous day in Genesis 19. Let's look at it carefully.

"*As Sodom and Gomorrah, and the cities around them.*" Sodom and Gomorrah were not the only cities destroyed that day. Deuteronomy 29:23 shows that there were actually four cities destroyed – "The whole land is brimstone, salt, and burning...like the overthrow of Sodom and Gomorrah, Admah, and Zeboiim, which the Lord overthrew in His anger and His wrath." When the Lord was reluctant to "hand over" Israel to greater punishment, the prophet said, "How can I treat you like Admah? How can I

---

[33] *The Epistle of Jude: An Exposition,* Kevin Conner, KJC Publications, page 31.

make you like Zeboiim?"[34] These four cities are together in the list of nations of Genesis 10:19 and the war of kings in Genesis 14:2 and 14:8. A fifth town, Zoar, would also have been destroyed had Lot not sought refuge there. Lot's presence prevented Zoar's destruction.[35] Although Lot was living only in Sodom, the sexual immorality and perversion had spread to other cities as well.

"*In a similar manner to these...and gone after strange flesh.*" The word "these" here is referring to the "angels" of verse 6, not the "cities" of verse 7, because "these" in Greek is masculine like angels and not feminine like cities. Thus, you can say, "In a similar manner to these *angels*." A few commentators think that these "angels" are then tied to the "strange flesh." Here are the words of two different commentators: "Thus the sin of Sodom and Gomorrah was seeking union with 'different flesh' in a way similar to what the 'sons of God' (angels) did (Genesis 6:2) when they mingled with 'the daughters of men (humans).'"[36] "As the angels fell because of their lust for women, so the Sodomites desired sexual relations with angels. And 'strange flesh' must mean the flesh of angels."[37] Genesis 19:4-5 makes plain that the "men of Sodom" had given themselves over to homosexuality, or "sexual immorality" as Jude 1:7 states. But if the "angels" of verse 6 are the "sons of God" of Genesis 6, then they had sex with women (humans), so "in a similar way," the men (humans) of Sodom and Gomorrah wanted to have sex with angels. This is certainly one possible interpretation of the phrase, "...and gone after strange flesh." The NIV translation simply uses the word "perversion." In summary then, what the angels did to humans in Genesis 6, now the humans tried to do to angels in Genesis 19.

However, most commentators believe the "strange flesh" is simply men going after other men instead of women. A man

---

[34] See Hosea 11:8.
[35] See Genesis 19:22-23, 19:30. Compare with Genesis 13:10 and 14:2. I believe the same is true today – The presence of Christian believers throughout the world is preventing even more judgments.
[36] *The Expositor's Bible Commentary: Jude,* Edwin Blum, Zondervan Publishing House, Grand Rapids, MI, page 184.
[37] *Word Biblical Commentary: 2 Peter and Jude,* Richard J. Bauckham, Word Books Publishers, Waco, TX, page 54.

Chapter 2: *Sodom & Gomorrah*

with a woman is "the natural" way.[38] The men of Sodom thought that the "two angels" (Genesis 19:1) were "men" (Genesis 19:5). That is, rather than seeking the "natural flesh" of women, they were seeking the "strange flesh" of men. Douglas Moo states it plainly: "Genesis 19 does not imply that the men of Sodom knew that it was angels they were seeking to have sex with. Nor is 'flesh' a natural word to apply to angels. Probably, then, the usual interpretation is correct: Jude associates God's judgment on Sodom and Gomorrah with the homosexual practices of their inhabitants."[39] This is probably the better interpretation. So whether "strange flesh" means "sex with angels" or "sex with men," the bottom-line is that it was homosexual sex.

"*Having given themselves over to sexual immorality.*" I'm always amazed at the consistency of Scripture. Remember when the apostle Paul speaks about homosexuality in Romans 1? He wrote, "God gave them up to uncleanness," "God gave them up to vile passions," and "God gave them over to a debased mind."[40] The reason the homosexuals of Sodom had given themselves over to "sexual immorality" is because "God had given them over" to the lusts of their own hearts. Contrary to pro-gay theology, which claims that Sodom and Gomorrah were destroyed because of a lack of hospitality, the Word of God teaches in Jude 1:7 that it was "sexual immorality." The gay rights movement calls homosexuality a "sexual orientation;" the Bible calls homosexuality a "sexual perversion." Thus, you read in Genesis 19:4-5, "All the men from every part of the city of Sodom – both young and old – surrounded the house. They called to Lot, 'Where are the men who came to you tonight? Bring them out to us so that we can have sex with them.'"

"*Are set forth as an example.*" Note the word, "example." 2 Peter 2:6, which I will cover in the next section, uses similar language: "God condemned the cities of Sodom and Gomorrah by burning them to ashes, and made them an *example* of what is going to happen to the ungodly." I have written this already, but I want

---

[38] As Paul says in Romans 1:27, "The men, leaving the natural use of the woman."
[39] *The NIV Application Commentary on 2 Peter and Jude,* Douglas Moo, Zondervan Publishing House, Grand Rapids, MI, page 242.
[40] See Romans 1:24, 1:26, and 1:28.

to repeat it: The destruction of Sodom and Gomorrah by the judgment of God has been set forth as a historic example of how God will deal with individuals, families, communities, states, and nations that embrace homosexuality. Early in the history of man, God established this fearful example, pattern, or model of how He will treat those who want to live in sexual immorality. When I see the liberal media – newspapers, magazines, TV, movies, and the Internet – celebrate homosexuality, and publish pictures of "happy" homosexual men and lesbian women kissing each other, I fear what God thinks! Our local, state, and federal governments have also caved in to the powerful gay political agenda and pressures. *For many, to reject the gay rights movement is political suicide. But I have a greater fear – to accept the gay rights movement is biblical suicide!* Be assured of this – we will experience the judgment of God!

"*Suffering the vengeance of eternal fire.*" Having just talked about "everlasting chains" in verse 6, now Jude is going to talk about the "eternal fire" in verse 7. Jesus taught that "the everlasting fire" was "prepared for the devil and his angels."[41] Quoting from Isaiah 66:24 – "A fire that is not quenched" – Jesus states five times in a row that "hell fire" is a "fire that shall never be quenched."[42] This again shows me the gravity and the severity of the sin of sexual immorality in general, and of homosexuality in particular. In similar language to the judgment on Sodom and Gomorrah, the apostle John says, "But the cowardly, unbelieving, abominable, murderers, *sexually immoral*, sorcerers, idolaters, and all liars shall have their part in the lake which *burns with fire and brimstone*, which is the second death." Sexual immorality has eternal consequences. Genesis 19:24 describes the destruction of Sodom and Gomorrah as "Then the Lord rained *brimstone and fire* on Sodom and Gomorrah, from the Lord out of the heavens." Jesus said in Luke 17:29, "But on the day that Lot went out of Sodom it rained *fire and brimstone* from heaven and destroyed them all."[43] It is grievous indeed to see certain strains of "Christian" denominations like Presbyterian, United Methodist,

---

[41] See Matthew 25:41.
[42] See Mark 9:43-48.
[43] Compare this with the wording of Psalm 11:6.

Chapter 2: *Sodom & Gomorrah*

Lutheran, and Episcopalian, not only embracing the homosexual lifestyle, but actually ordaining homosexual pastors, priests, and bishops! These groups that name the name of Christ have surely abandoned the clear teachings of Scripture. They are completely backslidden and have lost the fear of God.

Christians everywhere, let us not fear what worldly people may say about our position on homosexuality. In the name of Jesus Christ, let us boldly declare the judgment of God on Sodom and Gomorrah as God's example to all generations of how He will deal with homosexuality and ungodliness!

Sodom and Gomorrah in 2 Peter

2 Peter 2:6-8 not only affirms what is taught in Jude 1:7, it also allows you to see how homosexuality affects the heart and soul of "righteous" people. You are going to see that the sin of homosexuality grieves, oppresses, and torments God's people. It happened back then; and it is happening now. *Any Christian who is living for Jesus Christ will always be grieved by sexual misconduct.* If a Christian can see two homosexuals kissing, groping, and caressing each other, without some level of revulsion or disgust, then there is something seriously wrong. It's not because we are self-righteous Pharisees; it's because it is so unnatural. 2 Peter reveals that Lot's very soul was tormented and oppressed by the homosexuality that consumed Sodom and Gomorrah.

I should interject at this point that desensitization is one of the key strategies of the gay rights movement. In the now well-known article, *The Overhauling of Straight America,* two leading homosexual authors outlined a plan for how homosexuality can become acceptable in the United States. Listen to strategy #1: "Desensitization. Our goal is to desensitize the public so that it views homosexuality with indifference instead of with keen emotion. It's imperative that gays talk about their gayness as much as possible on TV and radio until people become indifferent to homosexuality. Straights will eventually be desensitized to the point that homosexuality will be viewed as just another lifestyle."⁴⁴ Here in California where I live, every major newspaper in the top ten cities of this state is solidly pro-homosexual. The news articles, pictures, commentaries, and opinions of these newspapers, always cast homosexuality in a positive light. Anyone who disagrees with this view is silenced and immediately labeled as "homophobic," "anti-gay," and "bigoted."

There are three fearful judgments mentioned in 2 Peter 2:4-6 – "The angels who sinned" and were "cast down to hell" (verse 4), the "ungodly" "ancient world" destroyed by the "flood" at the time of "Noah" (verse 5), and the "cities of Sodom and Gomorrah" "reduced to ashes" in the days of "Lot" (verse 6). Let's focus on what the apostle Peter says about the events of Genesis 19.

"And turning the cities of Sodom and Gomorrah into ashes." "After judgment by water, there is judgment by fire."⁴⁵ When the Lord destroyed the world by water at the time of Noah, He promised never to do it again by water. But after the Lord destroyed the cities of Sodom and Gomorrah, He did not make a similar promise. This will be Peter's argument in the very next chapter: "But they deliberately forget that long ago by God's word the heavens existed and the earth was formed out of water and by water. By these waters also the world of that time was deluged and destroyed. By the same word the present heavens and earth are reserved for fire, being kept for the day of judgment and destruction of ungodly men."⁴⁶ God destroyed the ancient world by water; God will destroy the modern world by fire.

To find the subject of this "turning," you have to go back to "God" in verse 4 – *"God* did not spare the angels." Thus, *"God* did not spare the ancient world" (verse 5) and *"God* turned the cities into ashes" (verse 6). It was the Lord who executed the judgment. These are some scary words. Think about this for a

---

⁴⁴ *When the Wicked Seize the City*, Chuck & Donna McIlhenny, Huntington House Publishers, Lafayette, LA, page 17. I recommend this book to every concerned and thinking Christian. It is the best book on homosexuality in the Christian market. It is prophetic and powerful.
⁴⁵ See the United Bible Societies (UBS) NT Handbooks Series commentary on 2 Peter 2:6 by Daniel Arichea and Howard Hutton.
⁴⁶ See 2 Peter 3:5-7.

Chapter 2: *Sodom & Gomorrah*

minute – God turned entire cities into ashes! The ERV translation reads, "He burned them until there was nothing left but ashes." The NCV says, "God destroyed the evil cities...by burning them until they were ashes." Ashes are the remains of a fire. It's the powdery substance left when something is burned with fire. Notice what Abraham saw the day after: "Early the next morning Abraham got up...and looked down toward Sodom and Gomorrah...and he saw dense smoke rising from the land, like smoke from a furnace."[47] A day later, the fire was still burning! It was truly reduced to ashes! Aren't we just a little bit afraid of what God can do to us? The judgment of God is awesome!

"*Condemned them to destruction.*" I thought "reduced to ashes" was harsh. This is very strong language. The Greek word here for "destruction" has come into the English language. It's the Greek word, "katastrophē," or "catastrophe." It means the total ruin and complete extinction of something. It gives you the idea of something so destroyed that no trace can be found afterward. The NEB is very accurate: "Condemned them to total destruction." The Jerusalem Bible says, "He condemned, He destroyed them completely." This is a frightening thought. And the English word, "condemn," is a Latin word that means "with damnation." Simply put, God damned Sodom and Gomorrah to absolute destruction.[48] The reason that these cities were condemned was not because of an earthquake or volcanic eruption. No, it was the ungodliness there. Hillyer is surely correct when he writes, "The reason for the catastrophe was the wickedness of the population."[49]

"*Making them an example to those who afterward would live ungodly.*" Like Jude 1:7, you again see the word "example." The destruction of Sodom and Gomorrah has been set up as an example of how God will deal with those who "live ungodly." The CEV reads, "This is a warning to anyone else who wants to

---

[47] See Genesis 19:27-28.
[48] It's only been in the last 20-30 years that archeological evidence has been uncovered that suggests these cities probably existed in the southern part of the Dead Sea. See *The Discovery of the Sin Cities of Sodom and Gomorrah* by Dr. Bryant G. Wood. They are truly extinct.
[49] *New International Biblical Commentary*, 2 Peter, Norman Hillyer, Hendrikson Publishers, pages 189-191.

sin." The NCV says, "He made those cities an example of what will happen to those who are against God." Again, let me reiterate, early in human history, God set up a judgment by fire as an example of how He will deal with ungodliness. Today, people laugh at sin, indulge in it without the slightest qualm, and mock those who want to live for God.

"*And delivered righteous Lot.*" This is one of the main points of this text. God destroyed the ancient world, but "delivered Noah." God destroyed Sodom and Gomorrah, but "delivered Lot." Therefore, "the Lord knows how to deliver the godly out of temptations" (verse 9). The wicked are condemned; the righteous are delivered. Proverbs says three different times, "Righteousness delivers from death," "but righteousness delivers from death," and "the righteousness of the upright will deliver them."[50] Remember in Genesis 18 that God told Abraham that He would spare the city of Sodom if He found ten *righteous* people there. By the sheer mercy of God on Lot and his family, once Lot left with his wife and two daughters, there were no righteous people left. I still believe this is one of the reasons God has not brought more judgment on the earth. We deserve more, but God's people are here. Recall Abraham's famous question – "Would You also destroy the righteous with the wicked?" Abraham answers the question himself – "Far be it from You to do such a thing as this, to slay the righteous with the wicked, so that the righteous should be as the wicked; far be it from You!"[51] Our presence holds back the judgment of God – but only for a season.

"*Who was oppressed by the filthy conduct of the wicked.*" In this and the next verse, you are now going to gaze into the heart of "righteous Lot." Specifically, you will see how the homosexuality in Sodom impacted his soul. The Greek word for "oppressed" is variously translated as "distressed," "sickened," "vexed," or "greatly troubled." It's interesting to me that the only other place that this word appears in the Greek New Testament is in Acts 7:24 where Moses kills an Egyptian taskmaster for "oppressing" an Israelite slave. What was it that oppressed Lot? It was the shameful, lawless, filthy, immoral and perverted lives

---

[50] See Proverbs 10:2, 11:4, and 11:6.
[51] See Genesis 18:23-25.

of the homosexuals. It was the evil manner in which these people were conducting their lives.

Many years ago, when my daughter was about five years of age, my wife and I were vacationing in San Francisco. Because of some construction on one of the main streets, we had to take a back way to get to the freeway. We got lost, and I turned onto a street that was lined with homosexual bathhouses! When I saw about fifty young, muscular men without shirts on the sidewalks jumping on each other and caressing one another, I got out of there as quickly as possible. When I wince or gasp at such a sight, people may accuse me of being "homophobic" or even "self-righteous." But I don't apologize: *This is perverted. This is unnatural. This is unbridled lust. This makes me very uncomfortable. And this oppresses my spirit.* I remember the famous quote by Cardinal Newman: "Our greatest security against sin lies in being shocked at it."[52] Few of us really comprehend the promiscuity that exists among many gay men. They can have sex with up to ten to twelve partners a night at these bathhouses. It has been reported in reputable magazines that 50% of the male homosexuals surveyed have had over five hundred different sexual partners, and those who are AIDS victims have had an average of eleven hundred (1,100) sex partners.[53] This is confusion. This is so contrary and foreign to God's original design of one man loving one woman for life. To say that I'm repulsed by this behavior does not mean that I hate gays! No, it's God who hates what they are doing because it is destroying them morally and physically.

"For that righteous man, dwelling among them, tormented his righteous soul from day to day by seeing and hearing their lawless deeds." Notice how Peter has described Abraham's nephew – "righteous Lot," "righteous man," and "righteous soul." I don't think anyone can read the Genesis account and conclude that Lot was righteous. As one commentator points out, "Describing Lot as a 'righteous man' may seem like a bit of a stretch. The Old Testament portrays him

---

[52] *The Letters of James and Peter,* William Barclay, The Westminster Press, Philadelphia, PA, page 327.
[53] See, for example, *The Gay Dilemma* in *Psychology Today*, cited in *When the Wicked Seize a City*, page 100.

as, at best, weak and compromising. He was rescued almost against his will."[54] When the men of Sodom wanted to have sex with the two angels in Lot's house, he did tell them, "Don't do this wicked thing!"[55] But then, he turns right around and offers both of his virgin daughters to these homosexuals to do with them as they pleased. And later, through the conniving of the older daughter, Lot gets both of his own daughters pregnant (Genesis 19:30-38). I will say more about this later.

Lot was found "dwelling among them." When Lot first separated from his uncle Abraham, he moved toward "the cities of the plain and pitched his tent even as far as Sodom" (Genesis 13:10-12). One chapter later, Lot is "dwelling in Sodom" (Genesis 14:12). Now I understand why Peter uses a Greek verb in the active voice – Lot "tormented his righteous soul." He brought this trouble on himself.

Not only was Lot "oppressed," he was also "tormented." This is a very strong word. The Greek word means "tortured," and it is translated that way four different times in the Book of Revelation (9:5, 11:10, 14:10, and 20:10). The TEV reads, "Day after day he *suffered agony* as he saw and heard their evil actions." I agree with Hillyer who writes, "Lot was worn down by being exposed day in, day out, to the vile manner of life of those who scorned the moral code and the law of God."[56] This was a daily battle for Lot. And it will be our daily battle soon. I understand what "seeing" "lawless deeds" means, but how do you "hear" them? When you apply this to homosexual behavior, you know what Peter is talking about. You could actually hear their perversions.

In summary, the apostle Peter gives you an insightful look at God's judgment on Sodom and Gomorrah, and Lot's suffering at the hands of the homosexuals who lived there. He was oppressed and tormented, but God eventually delivered him.

---

[54] See Moo, 2 Peter, page 105.
[55] See Genesis 19:7, NIV.
[56] Hillyer, 2 Peter, page 190.

Sodom and Gomorrah in Luke

The Bible is not made up of myths, legends, or "cunningly devised fables." It is the truth, and it is rooted in the history of mankind. The events in the Bible really happened, and historical documents, archaeological finds, and scientific data support its truthfulness. The judgment of God against the cities of Sodom and Gomorrah was a real historic event. Jesus spoke often of Sodom and Gomorrah as real cities, and their judgment as a real event.[57] Yet, some modern and critical scholars, who name of the name of Christ, openly deny, or doubtfully question, the veracity of this judgment. For Jesus, who knows all things and is the Truth, Sodom and Gomorrah were real cities destroyed by real fire and brimstone by the Lord God Almighty. And every time Jesus spoke of Sodom, it was always in the context of the judgment of God. And He used this judgment to warn us that a similar fate awaits cities that do not repent.

Like Peter, Jesus mentions the judgment of God on the world at the time of Noah and judgment of God on the cities of Sodom and Gomorrah at the time of Lot. Bauckham's comments are appropriate: "Since the Flood and the judgment of Sodom and Gomorrah are prototypes of eschatological judgment, the situations of Noah and Lot are typical of the situation of Christians in the final evil days before the Parousia (2nd Coming)."[58] In other words, what Noah and Lot, both righteous men, faced in their days, Christian believers will face in the last days. Noah saw much wickedness and violence; Lot encountered much homosexuality and perversion. As Christians in the "end-times," we will face these evils too.

I want to examine what Jesus taught in Luke 17:26-29. Here's what it says: "And as it was in the days of Noah, so it will be also in the days of the Son of Man: They ate, they drank, they married wives, they were given in marriage, until the day that Noah entered the ark, and the flood came and destroyed them all. Likewise, as it was also in the days of Lot: They ate, they drank,

---

[57] See Matthew 10:15, 11:23-24, Mark 6:11, Luke 10:12, and Luke 17:29.
[58] See Bauckham, 2 Peter, page 253.

they bought, they sold, they planted, they built; but on the day that Lot went out of Sodom it rained fire and brimstone from heaven and destroyed them all." I'm amazed at the similarities:

- "In the days of Noah"
- "In the days of Lot"

- "They ate, they drank"
- "They ate, they drank"

- "the day that Noah entered the ark"
- "the day that Lot went out of Sodom"

- "the flood came"
- "it rained fire and brimstone"

- "destroyed them all"
- "destroyed them all"

In one judgment it rained water; in the other judgment it rained fire. One occurred in Genesis 7; the other occurred in Genesis 19. The first destroyed the world; the second destroyed cities.

As a quick side note – it is here that you can once again locate the timing of the rapture. The day that Noah went into the ark, judgment came. The day that Lot went out of Sodom, judgment came. *And it's the day Christians get raptured that judgment comes. The rapture happens at the glorious 2nd Coming of Jesus Christ. It's on the last day, at the last trumpet, at the end of the age – not seven years before!* Further proof of this is found in Luke 17:34-36 when certain people are "taken" and others are "left behind." Where, not when, are these people left? Jesus answers in verse 37, "Where there is a dead body, there the vultures will gather." These vultures that gather to eat all the dead "left behind" are the very "birds of prey" in Revelation 19:17-21 that eat at the "supper of the great God." These are all the enemies of God destroyed by Jesus at Armageddon on the last day. And this is when the rapture occurs.

Chapter 2: *Sodom & Gomorrah*

While there are many similarities, there are some important differences. Note that in Noah's day, people "married wives, and they were given in marriage" (verse 27). This is not so in Lot's day. Maybe it's because the homosexuals in Lot's day didn't want "wives," but rather other men.

I think that verse 28 is a real warning for Christians living in our day. It reads, "They ate, they drank, they bought, they sold, they planted, they built." The NLT paraphrase says, "People went about their daily business – eating and drinking, buying and selling, farming and building." Notice what Jesus highlights. He doesn't say, "They were doing evil things, engaging in homosexual behavior, and committing wicked acts." No, *Jesus reveals that they were unsuspecting, unprepared, and living "business as usual."* Their whole focus was doing the everyday things of life like eating, drinking, buying, selling, planting, and building. The Lord is not against you preparing and planning for your earthly future; but it is far more important to prepare and plan for your heavenly future. Consider this thought for a moment. On the morning of Sodom's destruction, people went to the store to buy milk and eggs, cleaned their houses and swept their sidewalks. Men went off to work in the fields and stores. Construction crews were building new houses. Little did they know that Lot and his family were fleeing the city, because at noon, the entire city was destroyed by fire and brimstone from heaven! Spiritually, they were asleep. They were wrapped up in their sins and the mundane affairs of this life. Listen to this warning at Luke 17:30, "Yes, it will be 'business as usual' right up to the day when the Son of Man is revealed." We have been repeatedly warned: "You also be ready, for the Son of Man is coming at an hour you do not expect," "Watch therefore, for you know neither the day nor the hour in which the Son of Man is coming," "Be on guard! Be alert! You do not know when that time will come," and "you also be ready, for the Son of Man is coming at an hour you do not expect."[59] In Noah's day, "The people enjoyed banquets and parties and weddings right up to the time Noah entered"[60] the ark. *They got married one day and drowned the next. They took days to prepare*

---

[59] See Matthew 24:44, 25:13, Mark 13:32, and Luke 12:40.
[60] See Luke 17:27, NLT translation.

for a banquet or party but took no time to prepare for the judgment of God! This happened back then; and this is happening right now.

"On the day that Lot went out of Sodom it rained fire and brimstone from heaven and destroyed them all." Here in Luke 17:29, when Lot and his family "went out of Sodom," there were no more righteous people left. It didn't rain water; it rained fire. *That is a fearful thought – a rain of fire and brimstone that destroyed them all.* No one escaped. The ruin was total and complete. And Jesus adds in the next verse that this is how it will be when He returns.

Jesus said that this destruction was "from heaven." God did it. It was not the devil or an environmental disaster. For years, many well-meaning Christians have been trying to wear me down with tired phrases of how nice, kind, and loving God is. God is good. God is love. *But He is also a God of judgment.* I know a few Christian groups that will never attribute anything "negative" or "bad" to God. But the word of God is clear: "The LORD destroyed Sodom and Gomorrah," "we will destroy this place because...the Lord has sent us to destroy it," "the Lord rained brimstone and fire on Sodom and Gomorrah, from the Lord out of the heavens," "so God destroyed the cities of the plain," "the overthrow of Sodom and Gomorrah, Admah, and Zeboiim, which the Lord overthrew in His anger and His wrath," "God overthrew Sodom and Gomorrah," "God overthrew Sodom and Gomorrah along with their neighboring towns," "God overthrew Sodom and Gomorrah," and "God turned the cities of Sodom and Gomorrah into ashes, condemned them to destruction."[61] *God will judge the United States and any other nation that accepts and embraces homosexuality as a normal part of national life. It will happen.*

Now, I'm not hoping and desiring this to happen. I don't want nations, cities, or peoples destroyed. This is not what God wants. God takes no pleasure when the wicked perish, and God is not willing that any should perish but that all should come to repentance.[62] But people in Noah's day did not repent. People in Lot's day did not repent. *And people in our day will not repent.*

---

[61] See Genesis 13:10, 19:13, 19:24, 19:29, Deuteronomy 29:23, Isaiah 13:10, Jeremiah 50:40, Amos 4:11, and 2 Peter 2:6.
[62] See Ezekiel 18:23, 33:11, and 2 Peter 3:9.

Even after describing some of the greatest judgments in the Bible, here is the response of the people in Revelation 9:21, "And they did not repent of their murders or their sorceries or their *sexual immorality* or their thefts." I've had to learn this bitter truth – *Men and women are not converted by calamities. They are only hardened and infuriated more and more.*

I have a further conviction that I believe is rooted in the clear revelation of God and His ways in Holy Scripture. *Homosexuality will not continue to grow unchecked and unabated forever.* There is a point where God says, "Enough!" There is a point where the Lord draws a line in the sand that the wicked cannot cross. There is a point where the "sin of the Amorites reaches it full measure," "their sins are heaped up to the limit, and the wrath of God has come upon them at last," and "fill up the measure of the sin of your forefathers."[63] Our God is Lord, and He reigns in the heavens and the earth. He is the sovereign Lord of all history, and no one can tell Him, "Why did You make me this way or what are You doing?" *There has never been a civilization, nation, or empire that continues forever in wickedness and rebellion. The judgment of God prevents this from happening.*

Sodom and Gomorrah in the Prophets

After the book of Genesis, "Sodom" is mentioned in the Old Testament by name twice in the book of Deuteronomy, and then only in the prophetic books. Isaiah, Jeremiah, Ezekiel, Amos, and Zephaniah talk about this doomed city. Two main truths emerge – 1) The judgment that God brought on many cities and nations was just like the judgment He brought on "Sodom and Gomorrah." Peter was right again – "God made them an example of what is going to happen to the ungodly." 2) The sins of His own people in Judah and Jerusalem were just as bad or worse than the sins of Sodom.

The destruction and overthrow of Babylon (Isaiah 13:19, Jeremiah 50:40), Edom (Jeremiah 49:17-18), Moab and Ammon (Zephaniah 2:9) were just like when God overthrew "Sodom and

---

[63] See Genesis 15:16, 1 Thessalonians 2:16, and Matthew 23:32.

Gomorrah." The devastation of the judgment against Moab and Ammon was so great, that Zephaniah says these nations would be "overrun with weeds and salt pits, and become a perpetual desolation." The marginal notes of my NKJV Bible give an alternate translation as "permanent ruin" for "perpetual desolation." This confirms again what 2 Peter 2:6 says about being "condemned to destruction." It is forever ruined and desolate.

It is scary to think that the Jewish people, God's very own people, were sinning worse than the people of Sodom. In Isaiah 1:10, the Lord accused the "rulers" of being just like "Sodom" and the "people" just like "Gomorrah." And if it wasn't for God's intervention and mercy, they would have become altogether like these two wicked cities. The prophet Amos talks about all the judgment and correction God was bringing to His people, including being "overthrown like Sodom and Gomorrah" and "they still would not return to Me" (Amos 4:11). They persisted in their rebellious ways. Ezekiel 16:46-49 reveals that even the people of Sodom had not done as bad as His own people! They were worse. "Neither your sister Sodom nor her daughters have done as you and your daughters have done" (16:48). They were completely backslidden from God.

I want to look at three verses in the prophets that show what was happening in "Sodom and Gomorrah." In no particular order:

Isaiah 3:8-9 – "Jerusalem staggers, Judah is falling; their words and deeds are against the LORD, defying His glorious presence. The look on their faces testifies against them; they parade their sin like Sodom; they do not hide it. Woe to them! They have brought disaster upon themselves." As I read these verses, the thought that comes to mind is that these people had *no shame*. They were flaunting their sin before others without an ounce of embarrassment or disgrace. It's interesting that the word "parade" is used here by the NIV translation, followed by the words, "they do not hide it." Not only in San Francisco, but in many cities across the United States, homosexuals hold "gay parades" where they openly demonstrate their sexual perversions for all the world to see. They are so steeped in their darkness that they are completely unashamed. As Genesis 19 shows, the homosexuals of Sodom came out (all of them) to have sex with the angels who entered Lot's house. They were willing even to break down the door!

I remember many years ago going to the Golden Gate Park in San Francisco with my family. I wanted to take them to the Natural History Museum located there. Everywhere we turned at that park, men were kissing other men on the lawns, holding hands and hugging at stop lights, and even laying on top of each other in various places. There were open displays and exhibits of their perverted lifestyles without the slightest qualm. This is what Sodom was like.

<u>Lamentations 4:6</u> – "The punishment of My people is greater than that of Sodom, which was overthrown in a moment without a hand turned to help her." The prophet Jeremiah was grieved over the sin of the city of Jerusalem. Zion lay in ruins. Why would God's people receive a "punishment" that is "greater" than Sodom? I heard a minister say many years ago, "Judgment is always according to light." That is, the more we know, the more accountable we will be. If we do things out of ignorance, we are punished less severely. God deals with us this way. In Luke 12:47-48, Jesus said it this way, "That servant who knows his master's will and does not get ready or does not do what his master wants will be beaten with many blows. But the one who does not know and does things deserving punishment will be beaten with few blows. From everyone who has been given much, much will be demanded; and from the one who has been entrusted with much, much more will be asked."

Sodom was "overthrown in a moment." It happened suddenly. People didn't have time to prepare. It was too late to repent. Sodom was not gradually destroyed over a period of five years, where people could see the devastating effects, and then have time to turn from their ways and get right with God. God's judgments often come like "a thief in the night." It comes when we least expect it. The recent massive earthquakes in Indonesia and Haiti that killed 100,000's of people happened "in a moment." And it wasn't just that no one *would* help her; it was that no one *could* help her. No one could stop "fire and brimstone" raining down from heaven. Who can resist Almighty God when He gets angry? There was no help before or after. Before the judgment, it was too late. After the judgment, it was a heap of ashes. How can anyone help rebuild anything when all you have is ashes to work with?

Jeremiah 23:14 – "Also I have seen a horrible thing in the prophets of Jerusalem: They commit adultery and walk in lies; they also strengthen the hands of evildoers, so that no one turns back from his wickedness. All of them are like Sodom to Me, and her inhabitants like Gomorrah." Jeremiah 23 has God's "holy words" (23:9) against the false prophets and their empty oracles. These false prophets are "profane," "wicked," "evil," "worthless," and "prophesy lies" to God's people. The reason they "prophesy lies" is because they "walk in lies" themselves. They are speaking out of their lifestyle. I recall from my seminar on *False Teaching* that a corrupt lifestyle produces corrupt teaching. If you live wrong, you will teach wrong. If you live in darkness, you will speak out of that darkness.

The "prophets of Jerusalem" were just like the "inhabitants" of "Sodom" and "Gomorrah." The main spiritual leaders who should be speaking the very words of God were speaking the very lies of Sodom and Gomorrah. There was more than just homosexuality happening in these cities. There was "adultery" and "walking in lies." Remember Paul's words from Romans 1:25 that homosexuals "exchanged the truth of God for the lie."

When you have less than ten righteous people in Sodom, you will not have anyone opposing all the immorality going on in the city. There was no one to turn them away from their sins. There was no one showing them the right way. Like Paul said in Romans 1:32, "Who, knowing the righteous judgment of God, that those who practice such things are deserving of death, *not only do the same* but also approve of those who practice them." Jeremiah says that the false prophets were doing just like the people of Sodom – "they were strengthening the hands of evildoers." People in Sodom encouraged one another in their wickedness – all to their own destruction! The result was that "no one turns back from his wickedness." Malachi 2:6 reminds us that when the Levitical priests are doing their job, they "turn many away from iniquity." One of the ways that I measure the effectiveness of my ministry is I see how many people are turning away from their sins and iniquities. No one was doing this in Sodom. Truly, there were none righteous, no not one.

Today we see politicians, newspapers, musicians, churches, schools, universities, teachers, and professors strengthening the hands of homosexual men and women. They are encouraging them in their evil ways. As Isaiah 3:9 says, "Woe to them! They have brought disaster upon themselves." These are the people who truly hate them, because if they loved them, they would seek to turn them from what will bring disaster upon themselves.

Sodom and Gomorrah in Genesis

Genesis says more about "Sodom and Gomorrah" than any other book in the Bible. The Hebrew word, "Sodom," means "burning." For centuries, homosexuals were known as "sodomites." The literal definition of "sodomite" is an inhabitant of Sodom who practices the sin of Sodom, or sodomy. Sodomy is simply having anal intercourse with somebody. This, of course, is the common practice of homosexuals. Genesis 13:10 tells us that it was a beautiful place that was "well-watered" "like the garden of the Lord." But even though the geography was attractive, the "men of the city were wicked and sinning greatly against the Lord" (13:13). Beautiful place; wicked people. This describes San Francisco (in general) exactly. In the war of the kings in Genesis 14, the king of Sodom was "Bera" which means "son of evil," and the king of Gomorrah was "Birsha" which means "with wickedness."

Things were so wicked in these cities that people began to cry out to God against it. Genesis 18:20-21 reads, "Then the LORD said, 'The *outcry* against Sodom and Gomorrah is so great and their sin so grievous that I will go down and see if what they have done is as bad as the *outcry* that has reached Me.'" This outcry is mentioned again in Genesis 19:13, "We (angels) will destroy this place, because the *outcry* against them has grown great before the face of the Lord, and the Lord has sent us to destroy it." This is one of the key instructions that Christians can do at this time against the influence of homosexuality in our nation – *we must begin to cry out against it!* God heard this cry and took action. Are you crying out to God against homosexuality and gay marriage? Like Abraham praying for Lot, are you praying for people to get delivered from places marked for destruction?

The "two angels" (19:1) or "the angels" (19:15) that were sent to destroy Sodom are interchangeably called "men." These "angels" are called "men" by the people of Sodom (19:5), by Lot (19:8) and in this story (19:10, 11, 12, 16). These angels did not have wings nor were their faces glowing from a special glory. They looked like men. And the "men of Sodom" wanted to have "sex with these men who came in to your house" (19:5). Lot saw this as "wickedness" (19:7); yet, he foolishly offered his daughters to these homosexuals instead. This act of disrespect would later backfire on Lot because his daughters would have sex with him and become pregnant by their own father. When a father does not protect a daughter's virginity nor honor her sexual purity, it opens the door for the daughter to value her sexuality with the same value given by the father. If we dishonor our children, they will dishonor us.

When Lot tried to protect his two visitors, they pushed him out of the way and tried to break down the door. This is unbridled lust in full bloom. The angels supernaturally pulled Lot back inside and struck all the men with blindness. Genesis 19:4 reads, "The men of the city, the men of Sodom, both old and young, all the people from every quarter, surrounded the house." As I understand these events, when fire and brimstone rained down on Sodom the next day, all of the men were still blind. There is no indication that they ever recovered their eyesight. Is this not a telling picture of the darkness that these people were living in?

After "lingering" around in the house, and not sensing the urgency of the hour, the angels literally grabbed Lot, his wife, and two daughters by the hand and "set them outside the city" (19:16). After escaping to the small town of Zoar, the Word of God gives us some of the most fearful words ever written: "Then the Lord rained brimstone and fire on Sodom and Gomorrah, from the Lord out of the heavens. So He overthrew those cities, all the plain, all the inhabitants of the cities, and what grew on the ground." Lot's situation was very tragic. "In a moment," he lost his city, his sons-in-law, his possessions, and finally, his wife. Warned not to look back, she "looked back behind him, and became a pillar of salt"

(19:26). Jesus told us in Luke 17:31-32, "Remember Lot's wife! Whoever tries to keep his life will lose it, and whoever loses his life will preserve it."

Genesis 19:29 says that "God destroyed the cities of the plain, when He overthrew the cities in which Lot had dwelt." To overthrow a city means to pull it up from its roots and foundation, and throw it down to the ground. These cities were completely annihilated by the judgment of God. Early on in the history of man, the Lord destroys cities given to homosexuality and sexual perversion. This judgment has been set forth as an example of how God will deal with the ungodly.

In regard to sexual sins, the book of Genesis is no different than our day. You find rape, incest, fornication, adultery, and homosexuality. Dinah was raped by Shechem; Reuben had sex with his father's wife (Bilhah); Judah fornicated with his daughter-in-law (Tamar) who masqueraded as a prostitute; Potiphar's wife tempted Joseph to commit adultery with her; and the men of Sodom wanted to have sex with the angels. There is nothing new under the sun. Sexual sins are still wreaking havoc in our day. We are even seeing churches destroyed by sexual perversion of every kind.

O God, we cry out to You against the onslaught of evil at every turn. Lord, deliver us from homosexuality and gay marriage! Jesus, You alone are the Savior and Deliverer of Your people. Deliver us once again. Deliver us from evil and the evil one. As Isaiah the prophet prayed, "Oh, that You would rend the heavens! That You would come down! That the mountains might shake at Your presence – As fire burns brushwood, as fire causes water to boil – to make Your name known to Your adversaries, that the nations may tremble at Your presence!"

3

Standing Alone Against Homosexuality

"So the king of Israel said to Jehoshaphat, 'There is still one man by whom we may inquire of the Lord; but I hate him, because he never prophesies good concerning me, but always evil. He is Micaiah the son of Imla.'" (2 Chronicles 18:7)

Despite the Bible's clear warnings that "Everyone who confesses (names) the name of the Lord must turn away from wickedness" and "Do not be yoked together with unbelievers. For what do righteousness and wickedness have in common? Or what fellowship can light have with darkness? What does a believer have in common with an unbeliever?"[64] Christian believers, leaders, and Pastors are caving in and accepting the homosexual lifestyle and gay marriage. People who say they are Christians embrace tolerance

---

[64] See 2 Timothy 2:19 and 2 Corinthians 6:14-15.

but not truth; they call it "diversity" when the Bible calls it "depravity."

Rather than preaching the truth on this subject, these believers have become strangely silent. "We don't go there;" "we don't want to rock the boat;" "we are afraid of losing membership and support;" "we are called to preach love, not offend people;" and with many other spineless words, ministers like Joel Osteen and Beth Moore refuse to speak out. Paraphrasing the words of Jesus, "He who is not against them is on their side."[65] When we remain silent, we give them our support.

Some notable megachurches and their Pastors along with several Christian theologians and scholars have given in to the corrupt practices of the Lesbian, Gay, Bisexual, and Transgender (LGBT) community. Here is a small sampling of the compromisers:

- Pastor Ryan Meeks and the Seattle megachurch *Eastside Community Church* recently fully accepted every aspect of homosexuality. Pastor Meeks says, "I refuse to go to a church where my friends who are gay are excluded from communion or a marriage covenant or the beauty of Christian community. It is a move of integrity for me – the message of Jesus was a message of wide inclusivity." The church's clear message on video, audio, and social media is that they want "the future of the church" to be about "Jesus' radical love" that accepts every form of sexually deviant behavior.
- Dr. David Gushee is the Distinguished University Professor of Christian Ethics and Director of the Center for Theology and Public Life at Mercer University in Atlanta. Gushee declares that he now "stands in solidarity with the LGBT community." What he now believes is that Christians "need to reconsider the entire body of biblical interpretation and tradition related to this issue." He also concludes that there is no scriptural foundation for treating homosexual acts as morally wrong or evil. Thus, homosexuals and lesbians should be welcomed in

---

[65] See Mark 9:40 and Luke 9:50.

the church with "full acceptance" on terms that respect and honor their desires and deeds.
- One of the most popular Pastors in the United States is Andy Stanley of the NorthPointe megachurch, a church with multiple locations and tens of thousands of people in attendance each week. He is the son of the famous Pastor, Charles Stanley. He continues headlong down his slippery slope toward apostasy and depravity by slowly accepting more and more aspects of the homosexual agenda and lifestyle. He says that churches should be the "safest place on planet earth" for LGBT people. By this he means that you shouldn't mention anything about sin and repentance, but just show them love and acceptance. He also blasted bakery owners who refuse to make wedding cakes for homosexuals – "Bake the gay wedding cake and leave Jesus out of it," he demands. He has various homosexual couples serving together as greeters and ushers in his churches.
- Pastor Stan Mitchell and GracePointe Church in Franklin, Tennessee recently fully accepted the LGBT community and its perversions. We're "just people; we want no labels." They "express their love in the radical hospitality of Jesus who welcomes all persons regardless of sexual orientation." When Mitchell first announced his church's acceptance of homosexuality as right in God's sight and not sin, he was greeted by a 10-minute standing ovation by many members of the congregation. Others, however, soon left the church. The long-standing worship leader of the church (who is no longer there) was Michael Popham who had been married in California to his fiancé Josh Johnson. They were later married in Tennessee.
- Locally, a Gay Pride event here in my hometown was attended by an estimated 3,000 people. One of the leading groups in the parade (and carrying the massive rainbow-colored banner through the streets) were members of the First Congregational Church of Fresno. Lesbians from the church were holding both sides of the large banner.

What are true Christian believers to do when they see compromising Christians and churches, in the name of love, accepting an abomination to God? We are sending mixed and confusing signals to a watching world. Many reject the truth and accept the lie. They proclaim man's niceness, but not God's righteousness. What the Bible clearly calls "depravity," they call "diversity." Rather than let the Scriptures define us, they redefine the Scriptures. Rather than demand repentance, they demand acceptance. Of these people, Isaiah the prophet said, "Woe to those who call evil good and good evil."[66]

I believe God has a word for the church in this late hour. Actually, it's a question. It was posed to a good king named Jehoshaphat. He was a king who sought the Lord and removed idolatry from Judah. *But then he began to compromise.* He made an alliance with the wicked King Ahab by allowing his son, Jehoram, to marry Athaliah, Ahab's daughter.[67] Jehoshaphat ate and fellowshipped with Ahab. He even agreed to go to battle to capture Ramoth Gilead, a strategic city held by the Syrians. Here are Jehoshaphat's words of agreement to Ahab: "Why, of course! You and I are as one, and my troops are your troops. We will certainly join you in battle."[68]

This unholy alliance with an evil king brought the rebuke of the Lord. The Lord sent a "seer" named "Jehu" who rebuked Jehoshaphat with this question – "Should you help the wicked and love those who hate the Lord?" Jehu then added God's judgment: "Therefore the wrath of the Lord is upon you."

This is the convicting question that we must ask those Christians who are bowing to the wicked agenda of the LGBT community – *Why are you helping the wicked and loving those who hate the Lord?* Yes, these people, especially those who call themselves "gay Christians," are living a wicked and perverse lifestyle. Yes, these people hate the Lord despite their many claims to the contrary. These "gay Christians" are of the world. Notice what Jesus said about them in three passages of Scripture from the gospel of John: "The world cannot hate you, but it hates

---

[66] See Isaiah 5:20.
[67] See 2 Chronicles 21:6.
[68] See both 2 Chronicles 18:1-3 and 1 Kings 22:2-4.

CHAPTER 3: *Standing Alone Against Homosexuality*

Me because I testify that what it does is evil." "If the world hates you, you know that it hated Me before it hated you." "Light has come into the world, but men loved darkness instead of light because their deeds were evil. Everyone who does evil hates the light and will not come into the light for fear that his deeds will be exposed."[69]

What are true Christians to do with the ungodly flood of sexual immorality promoted by the LGBT groups? We stand. We resist. We fight the good fight of faith. We refuse to compromise. We embrace truth and love. Jesus is right. *Jesus hates homosexuality. Gay marriage is evil.* Paraphrasing the Apostle Paul's words in Romans 1:31 and 2:2, "Knowing the righteous judgment of God, that those who practice such things (including lesbianism and homosexuality, verses 26-27) deserve death, not only do the same but also approve of those who practice them. But we know that the judgment of God is according *to the truth* against those who practice such things."

In this teaching, I want to look at one of my biblical heroes. He was a man who stood alone. He stood with the Lord against a wicked king and his 400 prophets. His name was Micaiah. He was the son of Imla. *He refused to compromise.* He spoke only the word of the Lord. He chose rather to suffer for the Lord than to agree with those who were false. He stands as a great example of holy living in an evil age. May every Christian live like him.

There is Still One Man

The story of Micaiah's ministry is found in 1 Kings Chapter 22 and 2 Chronicles Chapter 18. God wastes no words. I believe his story is written twice, nearly word for word, because in the mouth of two or three witnesses every word is established. The Lord wants his story firmly established in our hearts.

After agreeing to join King Ahab in battle to capture Ramoth-Gilead, Jehoshaphat wisely told Ahab that they should get the Lord's counsel on how to attack this city and seize it. Ahab

---

[69] See John 7:7, 15:18, and 3:19-20.

THE CHRISTIAN & HOMOSEXUALITY

immediately produced 400 prophets. As it turns out, these men were all false prophets.

Amazingly, they all spoke the same thing. They all agreed together. They all told Ahab that he should go against Ramoth-Gilead because "God will deliver it into the king's hand."

For some reason, the words of these 400 prophets did not settle well with King Jehoshaphat. What these prophets said did not resonate with his spirit. Something was wrong. In 2 Chronicles 18:6, the king asks, "Is there not still a prophet of the Lord here that we may inquire of him?"

Ahab makes a statement that I think every Christian needs to embrace and make his own. He said, "There is still one man." Say that out loud – *"There is still one man."* This one man, by the power of the Holy Spirit, would stand against 400.

Here is what Ahab said about Micaiah: "But I hate him, because he never prophesies good concerning me, but always evil. He is Micaiah the son of Imla." These words are very telling. If the ungodly "hate you," you can be sure that you are doing the work of the Lord. If the ungodly love you, you are surely doing what is evil in God's eyes. This is the great dividing line.

While Pastor Andy Stanley (pictured) accepts more and more the wicked life of homosexuals and lesbians, his father, Pastor Charles Stanley is weathering an assault on all sides by the  LGBT community. The elder Stanley has had to hire armed guards and station them in the parking lot and the doors of his church to prevent pro-homosexual activists from entering his church and disrupting the services. He recently had to turn down an award from a Jewish group that wanted to honor him because that group received so much backlash for Stanley's position against homosexuality. While on the other side of Atlanta, his son, Pastor Andy, remains as popular as ever with compromisers and LGBT groups.

The words of Jesus and the apostle John are appropriate here: "Woe to you when all men speak well of you, for that is how their fathers treated the false prophets" and "For they loved the

CHAPTER 3: *Standing Alone Against Homosexuality*

praise of men more than the praise of God."[70] *If the wicked praise you, it means that you are doing wicked things. You are also in trouble with God.*

Micaiah was hated by Ahab because Ahab was wicked and Micaiah would never give in. The prophet always spoke words of truth. Ahab wanted to hear words that would tickle his ears and make him feel good. The king did not want to hear anything that would require a change in plans or lifestyle. Ahab wanted to continue in his evil ways.

As a royal official of Ahab's court went to bring Micaiah, the two kings dressed up in their "royal robes" and prepared themselves to receive the true word of God. They were at "Samaria," the capital city of the kingdom of Israel. They waited at the main "gate" of the city.

Once again, the 400 prophets "all prophesied before" the kings. One so-called prophet, "Zedekiah," "made horns of iron for himself" and said to them, "Thus says the LORD: 'With these you shall gore the Syrians until they are destroyed.'" Wow, that sounds official – "Thus says the Lord" coupled with an illustration using "iron horns." Surely, Ahab thought, this is God's word for me. As we read ahead to the end of the chapter, we soon realize that Zedekiah's words were lies. This was all a plot of a lying spirit that insured Ahab's death! Furthermore, "And all the prophets prophesied the same, saying, 'Go up to Ramoth Gilead and prosper, for the Lord will deliver it into the king's hand.'" That settles it. What further word is needed when you have 400 "prophets" guaranteeing success – and all of it "in the name of the Lord?" The two kings and their armies can go right into battle with full assurance of victory. However, Micaiah now enters the scene and he rains on the parade. What he prophesies will contradict everything already spoken. Micaiah will be ignored, but to everyone's peril.

What Micaiah Saw

Micaiah saw Ahab's future. It was not good. He saw that Ahab was going to die in battle at Ramoth Gilead. Micaiah saw

---

[70] See Luke 6:26 and John 12:43.

exactly how the 400 false prophets would deceive Ahab. Ahab's death would scatter all of Israel "like sheep without a shepherd." The prophet saw how "Zedekiah" would have egg all over his face when his prediction of victory would prove false. He would soon be found hiding in fear and shame in an inner room of some house. Most importantly, Micaiah saw "the Lord on His throne" sovereignly arranging all the events of the wicked king and his backslidden people. God was controlling the events of everyone involved.

This is very important. When "the messenger," Ahab's royal official, found Micaiah, he tempted him with a compromise. Everyone else was saying the same thing. This generates tremendous pressure on anyone else to conform, to adapt, to agree, to unite behind the popular, politically correct position. "Look, all the prophets are promising victory for the king. Be sure that you agree with them and promise success."[71] *It is the same compromise being proposed to Christians in our day.* Here was the compromise – *just say what all the other prophets are saying. Just agree with them and thus encourage the king.* "Speak encouragement." *Don't say anything negative. Speak what is good.* "Please let your word be like the word of all the others." Men and women of God, this is a test. Will you obey the Lord or give in to worldly pressures?

Today we have similar "messengers" like Matthew Vines and Justin Lee. Vines is an LGBT activist who wrote the book *God and the Gay Christian.* He produced a YouTube video entitled *The Gay Debate: The Bible and Homosexuality.* He  recently founded *The Reformation Project* where he seeks to convert churches to be more inclusive and accepting of LGBT. Lee (pictured) is the executive director of the Gay Christian Network (GCN) which he founded in 2001 as "a place for Christ-centered support" of LGBT people. Lee touts himself under the label, "I'm Gay & I'm Christian." Here's his basic ministry: To promote the virtues of the homosexual lifestyle to your church, seminary, Bible college or youth group. These two homosexuals, and many like them,

---

[71] See 2 Chronicles 18:12, NLT translation.

CHAPTER 3: *Standing Alone Against Homosexuality*

want churches to wholly embrace the gay lifestyle. *They are Ahab's messengers.* Just agree with us. Speak what is good about our corrupt way of life. Just say what other compromisers are saying.

Micaiah's response to the messenger was simple, yet powerful. "As the Lord lives, whatever my God says to me, that I will speak."[72] The prophet will only speak what God speaks. He will only say what God says. For Christians today, we must speak only "what is written." What is written is that Sodom and Gomorrah were destroyed by God because of homosexuality. The Lord "reduced the cities to ashes." Homosexuality is an abomination in God's eyes. God hates homosexuality. Paul said that God has given lesbians and homosexuals over to "vile passions" because of "lustful desires." The wrath and judgment of God comes upon such people and behaviors. People who live as homosexuals can never enter the kingdom of God because they are unrighteous. Everything promoted by the LGBT community is contrary to all sound doctrine. It is no different than "murderers, fornicators, kidnappers, liars, and perjurers."[73] Don't compromise. Don't give in. Speak what the Lord has spoken.

When Micaiah arrived before King Ahab, the king asked him if he should attack Ramoth-Gilead or should he "refrain." The prophet answered sarcastically, "Yes, of course you will win. The Lord is going to give you complete victory over them." The corrupt king didn't appreciate being mocked. "Ahab shouted, 'Micaiah, I've told you over and over to tell me the truth! What does the Lord really say?'"[74] Ahab didn't really want to hear "the truth." When Micaiah finally told him the truth in verses 19-22, Ahab ignored everything and continued with his plans. Many of us Christians claim to want to hear the truth about many things, but the truth usually cuts and convicts. Unfortunately, too many of us have our ears tuned to hear "positive lies" that only make us feel good about ourselves for a season. Solomon wrote in Proverbs 12:19, "Truthful lips endure forever, but a lying tongue lasts only a moment."

---

[72] See 2 Chronicles 18:13 and 1 Kings 22:14.
[73] See Genesis 19; Jude 1:7; 2 Peter 2:6-8; Leviticus 18:22, 20:13; Romans 1:26-27, 1:31-2:2; 1 Corinthians 6:9-10; 1 Timothy 1:9-10.
[74] See 2 Chronicles 18:15, CEV translation.

Micaiah now begins to tell both kings the vision that he saw. It was a vision of the immediate future. It not only included what would happen to King Ahab; it included what would happen to God's people. In verse 16 he said, "I saw all Israel scattered on the mountains, as sheep that have no shepherd." He adds, "And the Lord said, 'These have no master. Let each return to his house in peace.'" These words were fulfilled exactly in 1 Kings 22:36 when Ahab died in battle: "Then, as the sun was going down, a shout went throughout the army, saying, 'Every man to his city, and every man to his own country.'" God's people were leaderless. The head of the army, Ahab, was gone. They had "no master" and "no shepherd." They had no leader to show them where to go. Despite Ahab's many corruptions, his death further "scattered" the people of God. Everyone suffers when God's leaders don't listen to the truth.

This is happening in today's church as more and more Pastors and ministers of the gospel cave in to the LGBT agenda. If the shepherds give in, the sheep are sure to follow. Alexander Strauch has a powerful word on this issue: "As often seen in church history, weak, vacillating, doubting shepherds will be devoured along with the flock. Weak shepherds are no match for the deceitful spirits and doctrines of demons. The priests, kings, and leaders of the Old Testament who professed the law of God but did not hold firmly to God's Word, were destroyed by idolatrous religion. So, too, unqualified elders who were (and are) uncertain and uncommitted to the Word have done incalculable damage to the church of Jesus Christ. Because they did not guard themselves or the flock, many churches that once stood for sound, orthodox doctrine now reject nearly every major tenet of the faith. For if the spiritual leaders of the church do not cling firmly to the Word, what fate awaits the flock?"[75]

---

[75] *Biblical Eldership: An Urgent Call to Restore Biblical Church Leadership* by Alexander Strauch, Lewis and Roth Publishers, Littleton, Colorado, pages 180, 182. See also my teaching in the *False Teaching Seminar* available on my website where I address this issue.

CHAPTER 3: *Standing Alone Against Homosexuality*

The Lying spirit Before God's Throne

What truth can assure and comfort God's people in these troubling, evil times? What gives us confidence to face an uncertain future with faith and not fear? What encouraging word can we offer believers when it appears that evil men and their wicked schemes are prevailing on every side? The answer is found in what Micaiah saw next – He saw "the Lord sitting on His throne." This is it! God reigns. Righteousness will prevail in the end. Every evil thing, person, and demon will be thrown down. The Lord is sovereign. He is working everything out according to His great purpose and plan. His church will overcome and the very gates of hell will not win against her. If God is for us, who can be against us?

Not only was the Lord sitting on His throne, but "all the host of heaven was standing on His right hand and his left." It was a scene from the heavenly courtroom.

For people whose ears are not tuned to the truth, what Micaiah heard next in God's throne room sounds unbelievable. The Lord is actually planning Ahab's death and He wants the participation of "the host of heaven." Verse 19 reads, "The Lord asked, 'Who will deceive Ahab so that he will go and get killed at Ramoth?' Some of the angels said one thing, and others said something else."[76]

One of the spirits stepped forward and presented his ingenious plan. It was a clever plot that was sure to fool Ahab. "I will go out and be a lying spirit in the mouth of all his prophets." The Lord agreed with this strategy and immediately commissioned the spirit "to go out and do it!" The Lord added, "You will be successful." Ahab's fate was sealed. He was doomed to destruction. In the next verse Micaiah boldly declares before Ahab and all his lying prophets, "Therefore look! The LORD has put a lying spirit in the mouth of these prophets of yours, and the LORD has declared disaster against you." Sure enough, Micaiah never did say anything good to the king.

Will you be this bold in your day? Will you declare the love and judgment of God to this wicked generation? Would you

---

[76] See 2 Chronicles 18:19, TEV translation.

gladly suffer for His name's sake? Does the truth really matter to Christian believers? Yes, we must stand for the truth and speak it "in love" to a lost generation who desperately needs the Lord.

Not only did Ahab hate what Micaiah had to say, the false prophet "Zedekiah" did too. He slapped Micaiah right across the face and mockingly said, "Which way did the Spirit from the LORD go from me to speak to you?" Zedekiah was saying, "Do you think God would speak something like that to you and not let me know about it? I have the Holy Spirit, and I'm speaking the truth. Since when did He go from me to talk to you?" In other words, Zedekiah claimed that he had the truth and was speaking by the Spirit. Matthew Vines and Justin Lee are both saying that they are speaking in the name of the Lord Jesus. They both claim that Jesus is grieved by the "hatred" of Christians who oppose homosexual perversions. These types of people are not far from slapping us across the face. Is it possible that Vines and Lee are "lying prophets" sent to seal the doom of many homosexuals and lesbians who think that they can continue in their wicked lifestyle and still make it into the kingdom of God?

Micaiah told Zedekiah that he would soon be "hiding" in shame and fear in an "inner, secret room" when his false prophecy didn't come to pass. Deuteronomy 18:22 warns us: "When a prophet speaks in the name of the Lord if the thing does not happen or come to pass, that is the thing which the Lord has not spoken; the prophet has spoken it presumptuously; you shall not be afraid of him." Zedekiah spoke a lie. He would soon be covered in shame, having failed the king by not warning him of his impending doom.

How was Micaiah rewarded for speaking the truth to the king and his prophets? He was rewarded with a prison sentence! "Arrest him! Tell them to throw him in prison and to put him on bread and water until I return safely." *Never forget – The false prophets are running around telling the people, "Peace, peace," but the true prophets are in prison. Jeremiah was in prison. John the Baptist was in prison. Hanani the seer was put in prison by King Asa. Paul was put in prison. Those in prison have given living proof that they have not compromised. They have spoken the truth and have suffered.* Paul would write, "All who desire to live godly in Christ Jesus will suffer persecution" and "join with me in suffering for the gospel according to the power of God."[77]

I recommend that all Christians read Chuck McIlhenny's prophetic book *When the Wicked Seize a City*. The subtitle is *A Grim Look at the Future and a Warning to the Church*. It was copyright in 1993, but the events described in Pastor McIlhenny's book took place in the 1970s and 1980s. He pastored a church in San Francisco and he saw how the homosexuals and their supporters were taking over the political arena of this wicked city. His house was fire-bombed; he received death threats; he and his family had to flee the city to survive because the police could not guarantee his safety. Why? Because he stood up at city council meetings and opposed homosexuality. *This was in the 1980s*. Nearly everything that he predicted in that book has now come to pass. The only thing awaiting us is the active, personal persecution that will soon hit the Christians, Pastors, and churches who take a stand against the evil lifestyle of the LGBT community. Are you preparing yourself spiritually, mentally and emotionally for what's coming? I believe many Christians in America are asleep. They are asleep because they listen Sunday after Sunday to pop psychology sermons that make them feel good about their lives and future. Yes, Jesus is Lord. Yes, we are overcomers. But we must fight the good fight of faith. We must prepare ourselves for the hatred that will come against those who stand up for the truth. Read McIlhenny's book and get equipped for the perilous days ahead.

Even after being sentenced to prison and a diet of "bread and water," Micaiah was undaunted. He stood alone, but it was because the Lord stood with him! Micaiah was unafraid, unconcerned, and unworried. He warned the king and the people with these parting words: "If you ever return in peace, the LORD has not spoken to me. Take warning, all you people!" As one translation says, "Everyone mark my words!" These are fearful words from a true prophet of God. He may have been chained in prison, but his prophetic words were not chained. They came to pass exactly as he spoke them.

---

[77] See 2 Timothy 3:12 and 1:9.

Ahab Dies in Battle

Ignoring Micaiah's warning, both Ahab and Jehoshaphat go to Ramoth-Gilead and into the battle. Ahab would soon be dead, and it was a miracle of God that Jehoshaphat wasn't killed too. When you associate and join with the wicked, you are putting your life in real danger. In fact, Jehoshaphat foolishly obeys Ahab's directive as they prepare for the battle. Ahab says, "I will disguise myself and go into battle, but you put on your royal robes." No one in Syria's army would recognize Ahab as he went incognito to the fight. Jehoshaphat, on the other hand, would stick out like a sore thumb wearing the clothing of a king. As they say, Jehoshaphat was a sitting duck. In verse 30, the "king of Syria" commanded his "captains of the chariots" to go "only after the king of Israel." The king of Israel was Ahab.

As soon as these captains saw Jehoshaphat dressed as a king, they immediately pursued him. They quickly surrounded him and attacked. "Jehoshaphat cried out to the Lord for help," and "God diverted them from him." Jehoshaphat escaped when "the captains of the chariots saw that he was not the king of Israel" and "they turned back and stopped pursuing him." It was by the sheer mercy and grace of God that Jehoshaphat narrowly escaped. Using the words of the apostle Jude, the Lord had to "snatch him from the fire."

Proverbs 21:30 says, "There is no wisdom, no insight, no plan that can succeed against the Lord." Ahab thought he could outsmart and defeat God's decree for his life. We are not told exactly how he did it, the Bible only says, "So the king of Israel disguised himself and went into battle." Perhaps he removed his crown and put on the standard helmet worn by all the soldiers in his army. We do know that he put on "his armor" to protect himself from arrows and spears. Nevertheless, God knew exactly where he was hiding. God knew what chariot he was riding. God knew what weapon could be used to end Ahab's life. There is no escape when you fall into the hands of the living God.

CHAPTER 3: *Standing Alone Against Homosexuality*

"Now a certain man drew a bow (shot an arrow) at random and struck the king of Israel between the joints of his armor. So he said to the driver of his chariot, 'Turn around and take me out of the battle, for I am wounded.' The battle increased that day, and the king of Israel propped himself up in his chariot facing the Syrians until evening; and about the time of sunset he died." 1 Kings 22:38 describes further  the grisly scene of his bloody death: "Then someone washed the chariot at a pool in Samaria, and the dogs licked up Ahab's blood while the harlots bathed, according to the word of the LORD which He had spoken." We recall at this point the prophecy given by Elijah concerning Ahab because of Naboth's treacherous death: "Thus says the LORD: 'In the place where dogs licked the blood of Naboth, dogs shall lick your blood, even yours.'" Elijah and Micaiah's prophetic words were fulfilled because they were the true words of the Lord. Isaiah 14:27 says, "For the Lord Almighty has purposed, and who can thwart Him? His hand is stretched out, and who can turn it back?" Proverbs 19:21 says, "Many are the plans in a man's heart, but it is the Lord's purpose that prevails." Ahab died a tragic death. He failed to heed the warnings of the Lord. He thought he could outwit the Lord and His prophets. No amount of clever plotting can prevail against the Lord.

Despite outward appearances of toughness and sternness, can we state very clearly that the only person who really showed love to Ahab was Micaiah? The others lied to him and it led to his downfall. Micaiah opened the door to repentance.

This is also true of those who preach and teach the truth regarding homosexuality. Those so-called Christians who don't warn people living in this sexual immorality are the very ones who hate them the most. If we really love homosexuals and lesbians, we will warn them of the eternal consequences of their sin. Unrepentant homosexuals will spend eternity in the lake of fire. This is the sobering reality. The "I'm Gay & I'm Christian" belief will land people in hell, no matter how sincere they are. *Only those Christians who speak truthful to the LGBT community are showing the true, agape love of God to them.*

Standing Alone Like Micaiah

Many Christian believers are embracing the homosexuality lifestyle as acceptable in God's eyes. This is a great tragedy. These believers, rather than speaking the truth in love, they are speaking lies in hate. How can you let these lost souls go to hell without warning them? That's not love. If I do nothing when I see a small child moving toward a fire to put his hand in there, I am a coward and a derelict. I've abandoned all sense of right and wrong. *I must do something if I really care.*

I asked earlier – "What are true Christian believers to do when they see compromising Christians and churches, in the name of love, accepting an abomination to God? We stand. We stand against it. We refuse to give in. For the sake of our integrity, our future, our nation, our children, and our spiritual lives, we must maintain the standard of God's truth. Paul said it this way in Ephesians 6:13-14, "Therefore take up the whole armor of God that you may be able to withstand in the evil day, and having done all, to stand. Stand therefore, having girded your waist with truth." We "withstand" and "stand" in order to "stand" some more. And the first part of the armor of God is truth. The apostle John said that "through Jesus came grace and truth." Not grace alone, but "grace *and truth.*" Later on, Jesus would say, "I am the truth."

Elijah had to learn that he was not standing alone. There were 7,000 others who had not bowed the knee to Baal. And you need to know that truth in your heart – despite the many Christians who are compromising, there are many who are taking a stand. Nevertheless, be prepared to stand alone. Your family may turn against you. Your own sons and daughters may abandon what you taught them and embrace homosexuality. Your own husband or wife may disagree with you. *Stand alone.* Micaiah stood against 400 others. You can stand alone against those who are your family, friends, and co-workers. Once again, "If God is for you, who can be against you?" In other words, you are on the winning side.

Tony Campolo, Christian sociologist, pastor, author, social activist, and former spiritual advisor to President Bill Clinton, recently came out in favor of gay marriage and full acceptance of LGBT people in the life of the church. Why? In

CHAPTER 3: *Standing Alone Against Homosexuality*

large part it was because his own wife and daughter continually pressured him to change his views. He finally gave in! Like Eli the priest, who "honored his sons more than the Lord," Campolo will be "lightly esteemed" in the kingdom of God. The Lord said it was an act of "despising Him." Jesus said in Matthew 10:37, "He who loves father or mother more than Me is not worthy of Me. And he who loves son or daughter more than Me is not worthy of Me." John 12:43 says, "They loved the praise of men more than the praise of God."

Let's reject the weak, sentimental positions of people who throw in the towel rather than remain loyal to Jesus Christ. Like Micaiah, let us stand, and have done all, continue to stand!

4

Vile Passions: Lesbians & Homosexuals

"For this reason God gave them up to vile passions. For even their women exchanged the natural use for what is against nature. Likewise also the men, leaving the natural use of the woman, burned in their lust for one another, men with men committing what is shameful, and receiving in themselves the penalty of their error which was due." (Romans 1:26-27)

The *Uniform Code of Military Justice*, commonly known by its acronym UCMJ, is the foundational document of military law in the United States. It was passed by Congress on May 5, 1950 and signed into law by then President Harry Truman. It is *uniform* because it applies to all branches of the military. It deals with basically every conceivable legal matter related to the United States military. It covers court-martials, court of appeals, desertions, absence without leave (AWOL), espionage, disrespect toward a superior officer, aiding the enemy, insubordination, drunk on duty, robbery, damage or destruction of military property, and many other offenses.

When it was first written under President Truman, it also covered homosexuality. The UCMJ provided clear rules for the immediate discharge of anyone who was found to be a homosexual or who had committed acts of homosexuality. Much later, in 1982, President Ronald Reagan issued a defense directive stating that homosexuality was incompatible with military service and anyone committing homosexual acts or identified as homosexual or bisexual was discharged.

Everything began to change with the election of William Jefferson Clinton. In 1993, after much opposition in Congress, President Bill Clinton fulfilled a campaign promise and issued a defense directive that no service member could be asked about his sexual orientation. This directive eventually became known as "Don't Ask, Don't Tell." Homosexuals and lesbians could now serve secretly in the military without revealing their true identity. Nearly all senior military officers were strongly opposed to homosexuals in the military and expressed concerns that it would compromise the effectiveness of our armed forces.

On November 30, 2010, the Pentagon released a study indicating that a repeal of the "Don't Ask, Don't Tell" policy would have no effect on military readiness. Thus, in December of that same year, Clinton's "Don't Ask, Don't Tell" directive ended, and President Barack Obama signed legislation allowing homosexuals to serve in the military without hindrance.

At this point, the floodgates to homosexual perversion in the military were opened. Gay-weddings were performed at the military academies. Brigadier General Tammy Smith, the first openly gay general officer, was married in 2012 by a military chaplain to "her wife," Tracey Hepner, in the District of Colombia. Army General Randy Taylor was Master of Ceremonies at the Pentagon's annual Gay Pride Event, where he introduced "his husband," Lucas. In 2016, President Obama appointed 49-year old Eric Fanning, an openly gay man, as Secretary of the Army. Mr. Fanning, who thanked his young boyfriend for his unwavering support during difficult

CHAPTER 4: *Vile Passions: Lesbians & Homosexuals*

confirmation hearings, supports transgender personnel at all levels of the military. Last year, the present Secretary of Defense issued a directive requiring all senior officers (including General and Flag Officers) to undergo mandatory sensitivity training on Lesbian, Gay, Bisexual, and Transgender (LGBT) issues or face being dismissed from the military. Recently, the Vice President of the United States told graduates of the U. S. Military Academy at West Point that the military will be so much better with more and more "gay soldiers."

I served as an officer in the Air Force from 1983 to 1988 under President Ronald Reagan. If you had told me thirty years ago that the military, a bastion of predominately straight men, would embrace homosexuality wholesale, I would have not only disbelieved you, I probably would have laughed at you. It would have been completely ludicrous and preposterous to think that this could happen in such a short time.

In this teaching, I want to study carefully perhaps the most insightful and powerful revelation on homosexuality in the entire Bible – Romans 1:18-28. By the inspiration of the Holy Spirit, Paul reveals the true causes of lesbianism and homosexuality. How does homosexuality rise in a society? What is God's role when it does rise? How are true Christian believers supposed to think about homosexuality in our day? Let us learn from the opening chapter of one of the greatest letters ever written.

The Wrath of God

"For the wrath of God is revealed from heaven against all ungodliness and unrighteousness of men, who suppress the truth in unrighteousness." (Romans 1:18)

One translation reads, "God shows His anger from heaven against all the evil and wrong things that people do." Another says, "From heaven God shows how angry He is with all the wicked and evil things that sinful people do."[78] In three consecutive verses, Paul writes three important attributes about God – "The power of God" (v16), "the righteousness of God" (v17), and "the wrath of God" (v18). He is a God of wrath. The

---

[78] See the ERV and CEV translations.

word, "wrath," comes from an Old English word for "anger," and in this context it means "God's punishment for sin." It is God's act of judging. God punishes sin. He punishes "*ALL* ungodliness and unrighteousness of men," not just homosexuality. John Stott is right, "His wrath is His holy hostility to evil, His refusal to condone it or come to terms with it; His just judgment upon it."[79] Bruce says, "His wrath is the response of His holiness to wickedness and rebellion."[80]

Note that this wrath is "from heaven." This means that God Himself sends His wrath down as judgment upon men's sins. This is not from the devil. This is not because of bad luck. This really is *God's* wrath. Christians don't need to apologize for God's judgment. He is just and holy. He gets angry at sin. He pours out His wrath on all ungodliness and unrighteousness, including homosexuality.

Many of us do not even want to think about "God's wrath," much less talk about it. Paul had no such hesitation. He spoke a lot about the wrath of God in Romans.[81] In the very next chapter, he gives the same truth as here in Romans 1:18 – "But He will pour out His anger and wrath on those who live for themselves, who refuse to obey the truth and instead live lives of wickedness."[82]

However, we must not always view God's wrath in a negative way. "God's anger does not jeopardize His goodness; rather, it is a corollary of it, for if God were not angered by unrighteousness He would not be thoroughly righteous. God's wrath is thus not an aberration of His divine nature, but the result of holy love encountering evil and unrighteousness."[83] Another author agrees, "A man who knows, for example, about the far-

---

[79] *Romans: God's Good News for the World*, John Stott, Inter-Varsity Press, Downers Grove, Illinois, page 72.
[80] *Romans,* F. F. Bruce, Revised Edition, Tyndale New Testament Commentaries, Eerdmans Publishing Company, Grand Rapids, Michigan, page 79.
[81] See Romans 2:5 (2X), 2:8, 3:5, 4:15, 5:9, 9:22 (2X), 12:19, 13:4, and 13:5.
[82] See Romans 2:8, NLT.
[83] *Romans*, James R. Edwards, New International Biblical Commentary, Hendrickson Publishers, Peabody, Massachusetts, page 49.

CHAPTER 4: *Vile Passions: Lesbians & Homosexuals*

reaching injustice and cruelty of apartheid and is not angry at such wickedness is not a good man: *by his lack of anger he shows his lack of love.* God would not be the truly loving God that He is, if He did not react to our evil with wrath. His wrath is not something which is inconsistent with His love: on the contrary, it is an expression of His love."[84] If God didn't punish sin and wickedness, He would be totally unjust. "His lack of anger would show His lack of love." But because He is love, He must punish sin. He must discipline those who do evil. He corrects because He loves – "Whom the Lord loves, He corrects" is biblical.[85]

The last part of this verse is so important. One translation reads, "By their own evil lives they hide the truth." Our "evil ways prevent the truth from being known." Another translation says, "In their wickedness they are stifling the truth."[86] "Men, who by the evil which they do, prevent people from knowing the truth about God."[87] The Greek word, "suppress, NKJV" is a present tense participle, meaning that people "keep on suppressing" the truth about God. They keep "holding it down." By their wicked actions they try to hide God's truth.

Truth – The war we are fighting regarding homosexuality is over truth. What is the truth about homosexuality? It is not about diversity. It is not about letting people love whomever they want. No, it is a war over truth! What no one in the LGBT community will ever say is that homosexuality is evil. It is ungodly. It is unrighteous. In a few verses we are going to see that homosexuals exchange "the truth of God for the lie" (v25). And this is exactly what is so utterly wrong with Christians who embrace gay-marriage and lesbianism. "It's all about love," they say. This is false. Truth and love always go together. *When we mix a lie with love, it is always a perversion.* Paul will write at the beginning of Romans Chapter 2, "We know that the judgment of God is *according to truth* against those who practice such things" (2:2). It's not according to love; it's according to truth.

---

[84] *Romans: A Shorter Commentary*, C. E. B. Cranfield, Eerdmans Publishing Company, Grand Rapids, Michigan, page 29.
[85] See the teaching available on my website, *Whom the Lord Loves, He Corrects*.
[86] See the CEV, TEV, and NEB translations.
[87] See the United Bible Societies (UBS) Handbook on Romans 1:28.

Why is mankind guilty before God? "The guilt of humanity, then, is due not to a lack (want) of truth, but to the suppression of the truth."[88] God has revealed His truth to man – about Himself and His laws. God's magnificent creation (1:20) has revealed His majestic glory and awesome power. But man has suppressed this truth about Him. "The essence of sin is godlessness. It is the attempt to get rid of God."[89] "It is the attempt to suppress it, bury it out of sight, obliterate it from the memory; but it is of the essence of sin that it can never be more than an attempt to suppress the truth, an attempt which is always bound to prove unsuccessful in the end."[90] The truth about God and His ways is staring people right in the face; but they don't want the truth. They want to live their own way. They want to follow their own desires. *The God that they see is not the God that they want.*

God Makes Himself Known

"Because what may be known of God is manifest in them, for God has shown it to them." (Romans 1:19)

One translation says, "They know the truth about God because He has made it obvious to them," and another, "This makes God angry because they have been shown what He is like. Yes, God has made it clear to them."[91]

God delights to reveal Himself. He is the God who can be known. He wants you to know Him. In this first chapter it says that His righteousness has been *"revealed"* (v17); His wrath has been *"revealed"*[92] (v18); "what may be *known* of God is *manifest"* (v19); "God has *shown* it to them" (v19) "His invisible attributes are *clearly seen"* (v20) "they *knew* God" (v21); and they *"knew* the righteous judgment of God" (v31). In the next chapter, Paul

---

[88] Edwards, page 51.
[89] Stott, page 72.
[90] Cranfield, page 30.
[91] See the NLT and ERV.
[92] The Greek word for "revealed" in both 1:17 and 1:18 is the well-known, "apokaluptō," or "apocalypse." It means to "remove the veil; to uncover." In verse 18, it is the first word of the verse, giving it priority of place or emphasis.

CHAPTER 4: *Vile Passions: Lesbians & Homosexuals*

says, "We *know* the judgment of God" (v2). Note all the words – "Revealed," "known," "manifest," "shown," "clearly seen," "knew," and "know." Jesus Christ came to reveal the one true God. His creation reveals His majesty and glory. "Man knows deep down inside that there is a God."[93] "There is no uncertainty about what men can know about God."[94]

This is an awesome truth: *You can know God personally.* He wants to reveal Himself to you. In a very tangible way, you can know "His eternal power," "His Godhead," or "His divinity." In other words, you can know this amazing, breathtaking, and overwhelming God of love, compassion, mercy, and judgment. He created the most intricate parts of the smallest insect; and He unleashed with His creative word the largest galaxy in the universe! He is glorious in power. He is majestic in holiness. He is infinitely intelligent. *He knows everything.* He is Almighty God, and He can be known by finite human beings. And this is why Paul can write in the next verse that "they are without excuse." God is not hiding Himself from us.

What is the problem then? "They did not like to retain God in their knowledge" (1:28). They "suppress the truth" (1:18). Even though they "knew God," "they refused to glorify, worship, and thank God" (1:21). They rejected "the glory of the incorruptible God" and chose a dumb idol instead! What a scandal! It reminds me of the infamous words of Psalm 106:19-22, "They made a calf in Horeb, and worshiped the molded image (idol). Thus they changed their glory into the image of an ox that eats grass. They forgot God their Savior, Who had done great things in Egypt, wondrous works in the land of Ham, awesome things by the Red Sea." Instead of embracing the God who did "great things," "wondrous works," and "awesome things," they worshipped an image of "an ox that eats grass!" What an absurdity! How foolish!

This "exchange" in Israel's history is taking place today. "They *exchanged* the glory of the incorruptible God" "for an image of corruptible man" (v23), "they *exchanged* the truth of

---

[93] *The Epistle to the Romans,* A Commentary, Kevin J. Conner, City Bible Publishing, Portland, Oregon, page 38.
[94] See the UBS Handbook commentary on Romans 1:19.

God for the lie" (v25), so in their lives, "they *exchanged* the natural use for what is against nature" (v26). Lesbianism is an exchange. The foundation of homosexuality and lesbianism is idolatry – they have rejected the one true God (the truth) and accepted corrupt men (the lie). They are enamored with their bodies. They are consumed with their "lusts" (v24, v27). It's all about perverted sex. It's all about lusting after one another's bodies, and thus, they "dishonor their bodies" (v24).

The unprecedented rise in homosexuality in our day is because of the unprecedented rise of the rejection of God. Edwards is right, "The problem of human guilt is not God's hiddenness and therefore humanity's ignorance, but rather God's self-disclosure and humanity's rejection of it."[95]

His Eternal Power & Godhead

"For since the creation of the world His invisible attributes are clearly seen, being understood by the things that are made, even His eternal power and Godhead, so that they are without excuse." (Romans 1:20)

The NCV translation reads, "There are things about Him that people cannot see – His eternal power and all the things that make Him God. But since the beginning of the world those things have been easy to understand by what God has made. So people have no excuse for the bad things they do."

God is invisible. He is a Spiritual Being that cannot be seen with the natural eye. The Bible teaches that He is "the invisible God," "the King eternal, immortal, invisible," and Moses saw "Him who is invisible."[96] Romans 1:20 makes the startling declaration that what is *invisible* can be *clearly seen*. His power, glory and majesty are seen through the amazing creation. As one Pastor has written: "The creation of the world reveals that there is a God. The visible reveals the invisible."[97] Stott concurs, "The God who in Himself is invisible and unknowable has made

---

[95] See Edwards, page 50.
[96] See Colossians 1:15, 1 Timothy 1:17, and Hebrews 11:27.
[97] See Conner, page 39.

Himself both visible and knowable through what He has made. The creation is a visible disclosure of the invisible God."[98]

God has given mankind the knowledge and intelligence to make advanced technological devices and instruments that can see distant galaxies and observe the tiniest elements. *God's creation clearly reveals His eternal power and divinity.* David wrote in Psalm 19:1-4, "The heavens declare the glory of God; and the firmament shows His handiwork. Day unto day utters speech, and night unto night reveals knowledge. There is no speech nor language where their voice is not heard. Their line has gone out through all the earth, and their words to the end of the world."[99] God's creation reveals His glory. It "speaks" loud and clear that God is glorious. God has infinite power, infinite ability, infinite wisdom, infinite knowledge, and infinite glory. Psalm 147:5 says, "Great is our Lord, and mighty in power; His understanding is infinite." The Bible calls Him the "Almighty" nearly sixty times. He has "ALL might" and ALL power. Nothing is too difficult for Him.

Truly, "That's why those people don't have any excuse."[100] Men have corrupted many things and verse 23 speaks of "corruptible man," but there is "a witness which cannot be corrupted by man – the witness of creation."[101] We can know God. The creation allows us to "see" the Creator. The all-powerful God has made Himself known.

There are 10,000 different kinds of birds, 23,000 types of trees, over 1,000,000 different insects, 35,000 different species of spiders, over 20,000 different butterflies, 440 different sharks, over 30,000 species of fish, and over 2,000 different kinds of jellyfish. When you also consider the planets, stars, sun, moon, and the billions and billions of galaxies, it is all overwhelming. The sun alone is a marvel of God's beautiful creation – if it were hollow, it could fit 1.3 million earths! And it is one of the smaller

---

[98] See Stott, page 73.
[99] The phrase, "clearly seen," is a Greek present passive participle. This means that "it continues to be seen repeatedly." Thus, it matches David's words of "day after day" and "night after night."
[100] See the CEV translation.
[101] *Exploring Romans*, John Phillips, Moody Press, Chicago, Illinois, page 25.

stars in the universe! We cannot begin to comprehend the immense size and dimensions of the universe. *And God created it all.* The prophet summarizes it for us: "Who has measured the waters in the hollow of His hand, or with the breadth of His hand marked off the heavens? Who has held the dust of the earth in a basket, or weighed the mountains on the scales and the hills in a balance? Lift your eyes and look to the heavens: Who created all these? He who brings out the starry host one by one and calls them each by name. Because of His great power and mighty strength, not one of them is missing. Do you not know? Have you not heard? The Lord is the everlasting God, the Creator of the ends of the earth."[102]

Foolish Hearts are Darkened

"For although they knew God, they neither glorified Him as God nor gave thanks to Him, but their thinking became futile and their foolish hearts were darkened." (Romans 1:21)

One translation reads, "They know God, but they do not give Him the honor that belongs to Him, nor do they thank Him. Instead, their thoughts have become complete nonsense, and their empty minds are filled with darkness." Another says, "Yes, they knew God, but they wouldn't worship Him as God or even give Him thanks. And they began to think up foolish ideas of what God was like. As a result, their minds became dark and confused."[103]

This great and glorious God who deserves all glory and praise is rejected. More than that, we don't even thank Him for all the gracious and marvelous things He has done for us. When we fail to give Him glory, praise, and thanksgiving, we move from blessing to cursing, from fullness to emptiness, from wisdom to foolishness, from light to darkness, from the incorruptible to the corruptible, from holiness to uncleanness, and from love to lust. Rather than worship the God who knows everything, we worship man who knows nothing. "Men enthrone human reasoning and

---

[102] See Isaiah 40:12, 26, and 28.
[103] See the TEV and NLT translations.

CHAPTER 4: *Vile Passions: Lesbians & Homosexuals*

dethrone divine revelation. One result is the worship by man of his own ideas."[104]

What happens in this verse leads to what happens in verse 28 – "a debased mind." The word "debased" means "corrupted, contaminated, and polluted." This is the pivotal verse of Romans 1:18-28. Humanity's downward slide into moral depravity begins here. People, by deliberate choice, refuse to worship and thank God for Who He is. They reject God and accept an idol. They think they are advancing and making progress. They think they've become wise, but they've become fools.

When we don't worship and praise God for His greatness and power, four very negative and destructive things take place in us. These four things are found in verses 21, 22, and 23.

First of all, we become "futile (empty, vain) in our thoughts and imaginations." Our thought life becomes totally useless. F. F. Bruce asks, "From whence come these shameful perversions, this destructive hostility within the human family? It all arises, Paul says, from wrong ideas about God."[105] What we think about God is "complete nonsense" as one of the translations said. Let's just say it right now, though it may offend many, *homosexuality and lesbianism, men burning in lust after other men, and women involved sexually with other women, is complete nonsense! Worse yet, they claim that God endorses and accepts their sexual confusion.* It is senseless. It makes no sense.

Next, "our foolish hearts become darkened." We become fools. We start walking in darkness. When you walk in the dark without any light, you are going to fall, go the wrong way, and get lost. In the United States of America, we have lost our way. We are groping around in darkness because our hearts have become foolish. We take so-called "transgenders," people that were once known as perverts and sexually confused, and make them out to be virtuous and wholesome. Bruce Jenner, the former gold medal decathlon champion from the 1976 Olympics, has become the poster child for this foolish life. In 2015, after years of off and on hormonal therapy and vacillating gender identity issues, Bruce

---

[104] Phillips, page 28.
[105] See Bruce, page 77.

Jenner said that he was now a woman. He also made the preposterous assertion that he is a conservative Christian. Jenner's foolish heart has become dark. The great German reformer, Martin Luther, was right when he wrote, "The sin of omitting that which is good (God) leads to the sin of committing that which is positively evil."

The Wise Fools

"Professing to be wise, they became fools." (Romans 1:22)

Teenagers in their 2nd year of high school are known as "sophomores." This word has an interesting word history. It is made up of two Greek words – "Sophos" or "wisdom" and "moron" or "fool." The word "sophomore" literally means "a wise fool." This is the third bitter fruit that people produce when they don't glorify God and give Him thanks – *They become wise at being foolish.* I'm continually amazed at the evil creativity and corrupt ingenuity contrived with their dark minds. The NLT says, "Claiming to be wise, they instead became utter fools."

The Greek word "professing" is a present tense participle; that is, they keep on asserting how wise they are. There are so many famous musicians, singers, athletes, mayors, governors, teachers, "ministers," university professors, and television hosts who are "coming out" and letting the world know that they are "gay." They tout the glories of the homosexual lifestyle.

Anderson Cooper (pictured), the well-known television anchor for Cable News Network (CNN), came out in 2012 as a  homosexual. Although not married, he lives in Connecticut with his gay partner, Benjamin Maisani. He said, "I'm gay, always have been, always will be, and I couldn't be any more happy, comfortable with myself, and proud." Men are living in lust with other men. "The demotion of God and the exaltation of self give birth to a bitter irony – they become 'wise fools.'"[106]

---

[106] Edwards, pages 52-53.

CHAPTER 4: *Vile Passions: Lesbians & Homosexuals*

Where did this all start? Was it not the Garden of Eden? Was it not in the crafty mind of the devil himself? The serpent told Eve, "For God knows that in the day you eat of it your eyes will be opened, and you will be like God, knowing good and evil." Eve noticed that the "tree was good for food, that it was pleasant to the eyes, and desirable to make one wise."[107] As Edwards says, "Eve took the fruit which would make her wise and seeing, but she saw only her nakedness."[108] They thought they would be wise, but they became fools, and with one simple bite, Adam and Eve plunged the entire human race into a world of darkness, rebellion, and sin. We all have inherited the nature of a sinner. We all became fools.

The Horrifying Exchange

"And exchanged the glory of the incorruptible God into an image made like corruptible man – and birds and four-footed animals and creeping things." (Romans 1:23).

"Instead of worshiping the immortal God, they worship images made to look like mortal man or birds or animals or reptiles." Another translation says, "They don't worship the glorious and eternal God. Instead, they worship idols that are made to look like humans who cannot live forever, and like birds, animals, and reptiles." If you don't worship the Creator, you will worship something else in His creation. This is an important truth: "Instead of appreciating the glory of the Creator by contemplating the universe which He created, they gave to created things that glory which belongs to God alone. Idolatry is the source of immorality."[109] I want to highlight that last sentence – *"Idolatry is the source of immorality."* Once you take your eyes off the Creator, you will put them on the creature. Rather than gaze at the unfading beauty of the incorruptible God, you gaze at the fading beauty of corruptible man. The idolatry opens the door to the immorality.

---

[107] See Genesis 3:5-6.
[108] Edwards page 53.
[109] Bruce, pages 77-78.

This is the fourth result of Romans 1:21: When you don't honor and worship God, you end up in idol worship, and the idols become our bodies that are dishonored among us. *The root cause of homosexuality is idolatry.* Lesbians do not love God; they lust after other women, doing what is unnatural. Homosexuals do not love God; they lust after other men, doing what is shameful.

The key word for the next few verses is the word, "exchange." "They *exchange* the truth of God for the lie" (v25) and "even their women *exchange* the natural use for what is against nature" (v26). There is a *trade* involved. The NCV translation of verse 24 reads, "They *traded* the glory of God who lives forever for the worship of idols made to look like earthly people, birds, animals, and snakes." Sports teams trade players – one athlete for another. Collectors and fans trade baseball cards. My dictionary defines "trade" as "to exchange; an exchange of somebody or something for another." Foolish men and women have traded the Lord in for a man or something from the animal creation. Earlier we quoted from Psalm 106: "Thus they *changed* their glory into the image of an ox that eats grass. They forgot God their Savior, Who had done great things in Egypt" (verses 21-22). They traded God in for "the image of an ox!" The Psalm writer was recalling the terrible sin when Israel "made a calf in Horeb, and worshiped the molded image" (verse 19). Wiersbe sums it up well: "Man exchanged the glory of the true God for substitute gods that he himself made. He exchanged glory for shame, incorruption for corruption, truth for lies."[110]

The utter foolishness of man is seen in this verse. He exchanges God for something corrupt like man, but it doesn't stop there. It goes from "birds," who are high in the sky; to animals, who walk on the ground; to finally, "creeping things," that are in the ground. Man gets progressively lower and lower. He starts with man, God's highest creation, and he ends up with a bug that crawls around in the ground! And he considers that wisdom! This is pure foolishness. All over the world, people are worshipping idols made by man's hands. As Wiersbe says again, man stoops

---

[110] *Be Right: Romans*, Warren Wiersbe, The BE Series Commentary, David C. Cook Publishers, see notes on Romans 1:24.

"so low so as to worship birds, beasts, and bugs!"[111] This is shocking!

God Gave Them Up

"Therefore God also gave them up to uncleanness, in the lusts of their hearts, to dishonor their bodies among themselves." (Romans 1:24)

I like the wording of several different translations: "So God let these people go their own way. They did what they wanted to do, and their filthy thoughts made them do shameful things with their bodies." "So God let them go ahead into every sort of sex sin, and do whatever they wanted to – yes, vile and sinful things with each other's bodies."[112] One commentator says, "Their wish becomes their punishment. It is awesome to consider that God hands people over to the evils they desire."[113]

The rise of homosexuality in our day is the direct result of God giving us over to our own depraved and warped sexual desires. "Those who abandon God find themselves abandoned by God at last. He gives men up to their own way, and a terrible way it is."[114] We are reaping a terrible harvest of bitter fruit. We are sowing to the wind and we are going to reap a whirlwind. God's wrath does not just mean natural disasters like earthquakes, tsunamis, and hurricanes that destroy buildings and take lives, but it includes the Lord leaving us to ourselves – we will destroy one another. "God's wrath operates not by God's intervention but precisely by His not intervening, by letting men and women go their own way."[115] I agree with another commentator who says: "When God visits His wrath in the way described in this passage there is no divine cataclysm and no fire from on high sent to consume sinful society. Rather, the wrath which God visits on sinful humanity consists in simply letting humanity have its own way."[116]

---

[111] See Wiersbe's commentary again on Romans 1:24.
[112] See the CEV and TLB translations.
[113] Edwards, page 54.
[114] Phillips, page 32.
[115] John Ziesler, quoted by Stott, page 75.
[116] Achtemeier, page 40.

I'm reminded of the ominous words of the Psalmist who wrote, "They lusted exceedingly in the wilderness, and tested God in the desert. *So God gave them what they asked for*, but instead sent a wasting disease upon them." This is the most dangerous and frightening place to find ourselves – when God gives us over to our evil cravings and desires. We will be completely overrun by them. Our own lusts dominate us and take over our lives. No doubt, the unprecedented rise of so called "addictions" – sexual, drug, alcohol – is due in large part to God abandoning us to our appetites and passions. C. S. Lewis said, "The lost enjoy forever the horrible freedom they have demanded, and are therefore self-enslaved."[117]

This is especially true of our sexuality. The fearful words of Jude 1:7 describe what it was like when homosexuality overran Sodom and Gomorrah – they "having given themselves over to sexual immorality." *They gave themselves over because God gave them over*. They no longer had any restraint. They lost all self-control. The apostle Paul describes this way of life perfectly: "They have no sense of shame. They have *given themselves over* to sensuality so as to indulge in every kind of impurity, with a continual lust for more."[118]

Note carefully what God has given us over to – "uncleanness." What do you get when you add "uncleanness," "lusts," and physical "bodies?" It equals sexual immorality. You get pornography, fornication, adultery, incest, homosexuality, bisexuality, and transgenderism. You get sexual confusion and perversion. In verses like 2 Corinthians 12:21, Galatians 5:19, Ephesians 5:3, Colossians 3:5, and 1 Thessalonians 4:7 we find "uncleanness" listed with sexual sins like adultery, fornication, and lasciviousness. Uncleanness represents sexual sin, and God has given people over to lesbianism and homosexuality (1:26-27).

---

[117] *The Problem of Pain*, C. S. Lewis, HarperOne Publishers, San Francisco, California, page 115.
[118] See Ephesians 4:18. This quote combines the NLT and NIV translations.

From Truth to Lies

"Who exchanged the truth of God for the lie, and worshiped and served the creature rather than the Creator, who is blessed forever. Amen." (Romans 1:25)

The Message Paraphrase reads, "They worshiped the god they made instead of the God who made them." What wording! Other translations say, "Instead of believing what they knew was the truth about God, they deliberately chose to believe lies." "They worshiped God's creation instead of God."[119] The thought behind these words is "they worship and serve what God has made; they do not worship and serve the very One who made everything."[120]

"Verse 25 repeats the thought of verse 23, that exchanging the truth for a lie is the root of idolatry. Idolatry paves the way for persons to destroy themselves and society. It turns creation into chaos."[121] "We reach now the climax of man's battle with God's truth when man exchanges the truth of God for 'the lie' and abandons truth completely. 'The lie' is that man is his own god, and he should worship and serve himself and not the Creator."[122]

This is now the second "exchange." First, men exchanged (traded) God's glory for an image. They reduced God down to an image they could see. They created "a god" in their own image. Now they've exchanged (traded) the truth of God for the lie. The wording in the Greek text is clearly "for THE lie." What is THE lie? The rest of verse 25 gives the answer – "They worshipped and served the creature rather than the Creator." "The lie means the whole futility of idolatry."[123] As one of the translations said, "They worshipped God's creation instead of God." The truth is that the one true and living God is awesome in glory, power,

---

[119] See the TLB and CEV translations.
[120] *A Handbook on Paul's Letter to the Romans*, B. W. Newman and E. A. Nida, United Bible Society (UBS) translators, notes on Romans 1:25.
[121] Edwards, pages 54-55.
[122] See Wiersbe's commentary on Romans 1:25.
[123] Cranfield, page 35.

majesty, and holiness, and once you reject Him – His Word, His truth, and His glory – people plunge into darkness and lies.

What does all of this have to do with homosexuality? Stott is surely correct when he writes, "The history of the world confirms that idolatry tends to immorality. A false image of God leads to a false understanding of sex."[124] The cultural war over homosexuality and lesbianism is a war over truth. Homosexuality is a lie. It is an abomination. It is evil. It is perverted. It is shameful. It is vile. It is corrupt. It is wicked. *It is not about equal rights, civil rights, or diversity.* It is about truth. There will never be peace. We can never arrive at a truce. The Word of God will always be at war with homosexuality. Paul's words from Galatians 5:17 are appropriate here: "The sinful self (flesh) wants what is against the Spirit, and the Spirit wants what is against the sinful self. They are always fighting against each other."

What you believe will determine how you live. If you believe a lie, your life will be a lie. "For once people stop believing in the truth, they do not believe in nothing, they believe in anything!"[125] Once you reject the truth, anything goes. Any sexually perverse lifestyle is acceptable – women with women, men with men, men with men and women, and men who think they are women and women who think they are men. The truth of God says this is confusion. *They live as if there is no God.* But just because God delays His judgment, it doesn't mean that judgment will never come. In His mercy, God is giving us the opportunity to repent.

On February 15, 2015, Lieutenant Governor Kate Brown (pictured) became the first bisexual governor of any state. She  became governor because of the resignation of Dr. John Kitzhaber, the longest-serving governor in Oregon history. Kitzhaber was engulfed in a scandal regarding his live-in girlfriend. Governor Brown is a lesbian, but she's married to Dan Little, her husband since 1997. The LGBT community calls her a "half-queer," by her own

---

[124] Stott, page 76.
[125] G. K. Chesterton, quoted by Edwards, page 49.

CHAPTER 4: *Vile Passions: Lesbians & Homosexuals*

admission. By definition, a bisexual is someone who is sexually attracted to both men and women, or engaging in both heterosexual and homosexual activity. *It never ceases to amaze me that people who cannot even govern their own lives are elected to govern a state!* But in the socially liberal state of Oregon, anything is possible.

The Lesbian Verse

"For this reason God gave them up to vile passions. For even their women exchanged the natural use for what is against nature." (Romans 1:26)

This is the only verse in the Bible that speaks explicitly about lesbians. Eugene Peterson's *Message* Paraphrase provides this interesting wording of verses 26-27: "Refusing to know God, they soon didn't know to be human either – women didn't know how to be women, men didn't know how to be men. Sexually confused, they abused and defiled one another, women with women, and men with men – all lust, no love." Other translations say, "That is why God abandoned them to their shameful desires. Even the women turned against the natural way to have sex and instead indulged in sex with each other." "Because people did those things, God left them and let them do the shameful things they wanted to do. Women stopped having natural sex with men and started having sex with other women." "That is why God let go of them and let them do all these evil things, so that even their women turned against God's natural plan for them and indulged in sex sin with each other."

The Bible calls the lesbian lifestyle a "vile passion." The Greek word here for "passion" (pathos) is used only three times in the entire NT, and all references are about sexual sin.[126] These are the "lusts of their hearts" of verse 24. "Vile" or "atimia" is a Greek noun that means "shame, contempt, or dishonor." Paul will use this word later in Romans 9:21-22 to speak of *"dishonorable vessels"* that are marked out for God's wrath and destruction. No one can ever say that the apostle Paul endorsed lesbianism.

---

[126] Besides this verse, see Colossians 3:5 and 1 Thessalonians 4:5.

"God gave them up" in verse 24 and He "gives them up" again in verse 26. When women reject the "Creator," they begin to worship the "creature." Lesbians don't want God; they want other women. As one early church father said, "God gave them up because that is what they wanted."[127] Because they "exchanged" God's glory into an image, and they "exchanged" the truth of God for the lie, the consequence is that they will "exchange" what is "natural" for what is "against nature." This is now our third exchange. This is why we have lesbians today – They have rejected God so God has given them over to their "vile passions."

These words, "natural" and "nature" are very important. The Greek word is "phusin." As one author explains this word: "Natural means God's created order. To act 'against nature' means to violate the order which God has established, whereas to act 'according to nature' means to behave 'in accordance with the intention of the Creator.'"[128] Another says, "Paul cites lesbianism not because it is a worse sin but because it exemplifies better than other sins the very nature of sin, which is the perversion of an original good, and hence idolatry."[129] Thus, it is "the exchanging of something authentic for something counterfeit."[130] In other words, *if you want to see the true nature of sin, just look at lesbianism; it is a corruption of God's original design.* The UBS translators, when giving instruction on how this verse should be translated from the original Greek to other languages, provide this advice: "The second sentence in verse 26 may simply be translated as 'women have sexual relations with women, which is not the way it should be.' This final phrase is simply a way of indicating the unnatural character of such acts."[131]

A minister friend wrote these insightful words on this issue of what "natural" means – "If homosexuality's origin is natural, that is, from birth, one would expect, as with other

---

[127] *Ancient Commentary on Scripture, Romans, Volume VI,* Edited by Gerald Bray, statement by Oecumenius, Inter-Varsity Press, Downers Grove, Illinois, page 47.
[128] Scott, page 75.
[129] Edwards, page 55.
[130] Ibid, page 55.
[131] See the UBS translation notes on Romans 1:26.

CHAPTER 4: *Vile Passions: Lesbians & Homosexuals*

naturally inherited traits such as gender and race, that such traits continue unchanged through a lifetime and are passed on to the next generation. Naturally inherited traits are unchangeable. A male remains a male his entire lifetime; a female remains a female her entire lifetime. Further, males and females reproduce their own kind, namely, other males and females. Reproduction after one's kind is a characteristic of all species. As with gender, the same is true of race. Hispanics remain such their entire lifetime as do Blacks, Asians, Caucasians, and all other races. Further, Hispanics reproduce their own kind, namely, other Hispanics. Blacks, Asians, Caucasians do likewise – they reproduce their own kind. If homosexuality is in the same category as gender and race, why do homosexuals not reproduce homosexuals – naturally? If homosexuality were a naturally inherited trait from birth one would expect they would. Clearly homosexuality is a choice, not a condition. In contrast, race and gender is a condition not a choice."[132] This is true!

There are some well-known lesbians – Ellen DeGeneres (pictured), Jodie Foster, Rosie O'Donnell, and Jane Lynch, just to name a few. Even a cursory look into these women's lives reveal the confusion and disorientation. Ellen was initially a sexual partner with Anne Heche, but that only lasted a few years, before she moved in with lesbian, Alexandra Hedison. Hedison left Ellen in 2004 and ended up marrying actress, Jodie Foster. Ellen then married Australian model, Portia de Rossi in  2008. De Rossi was dumped by her husband, Mel Metcalfe, for his brother's wife. This adulterous act broke up both marriages. De Rossi then moved in with lesbian partner, Francesca Gregorini, an Italian director and writer, but the relationship only last a few years. Now she's married to Ellen. O'Donnell married fellow lesbian partner, Kelli Carpenter, in 2004, when then San Francisco mayor, Gavin Newsom, permitted marriage licenses to be granted to same-sex couples despite California's laws at that time forbidding such unions. The "marriage" was annulled the same

---

[132] Taken from the article, *Homosexuality: How Natural? How Healthy?* by Dr. John Amstutz.

year. O'Donnell remarried in 2012 to Michelle Rounds, but that marriage ended in divorce in 2015. Does anyone sense the happiness and joy in these lesbian relationships?

Men With Men

"Likewise also the men, leaving the natural use of the woman, burned in their lust for one another, men with men committing what is shameful, and receiving in themselves the penalty of their error which was due." (Romans 1:27)

Some translations render this verse as follows: "In the same way the men also abandoned natural relations with women and were inflamed with lust for one another. Men committed indecent acts with other men, and received in themselves the due penalty for their perversion." "Men behaved in the same way. They stopped wanting to have sex with women and had strong desires for sex with other men. They did shameful things with each other, and what has happened to them is punishment for their foolish deeds."[133] One translation ends with "the fitting wage of such perversion."

This verse starts out with "likewise also the men." The men did what the women did. The women went after other women; the men after other men. They went after the "same-sex."

Next, we read, "...leaving the natural use of the woman." The previous verse had "natural use," and now we see it again. Simply put, it is natural for a man to be with a woman; it is unnatural, or against nature, for a man to be with another man.

From the beginning we had Adam and Eve, or male and female. When the animals came to the ark, they came in pairs as "male and female." Noah had his wife. His three sons had their three "female" wives. The only way that humans and animals could continue to propagate was through relationships between "male and female." Afterwards, God's law would state clearly in Leviticus 18:22 and 20:13, "Do not practice homosexuality, having sex with another man as with a woman. It is a detestable sin." "If a man practices homosexuality, having sex with another

---

[133] See the NIV and CEV translations. The last phrase was taken from the NEV.

man as with a woman, both men have committed a detestable act. They must both be put to death, for they are guilty of a capital offense."

Continuing on, these men "burned in lust for one another." Chrysostom wrote many centuries ago, "For he does not say that they were enamored (in love) of one another but that they were consumed by lust for one another."[134] Wiersbe writes, "This is the meaning of Romans 1:18, 'The wrath of God is being revealed from heaven' (literal translation). God revealed His wrath, not by sending fire from heaven, but by abandoning sinful men to their lustful ways."[135] We have here "the abandonment of men to their lusts" and "once lust is unbridled, it knows no limit."[136]

"Men with men committing what is shameful." Homosexuality is full of shame. Despite the current widespread acceptance of homosexuality in many cultures, there is still an enormous amount of shame in the life of the homosexual. Let's just say it – homosexuality is disgraceful and embarrassing. Most homosexuals, if they are honest, still have a great struggle "coming out" and living openly as a "gay man." The struggle is just this – *what he is doing is shameful*.

Finally, "...and receiving in themselves the penalty of their error which was due." I was immediately drawn to the word, "error." The main Greek verb in the NT for "deceive" or "go astray" is "planaō." It's where we get our English word for "planet." Planaō comes directly from "planē," the word translated here for "error." Homosexual men are going to "receive a penalty." They are deceived. They have gone astray. The word here for "error" could also be translated "delusion." The apostle Paul uses the same Greek word in 2 Thessalonians 2:11, "And for this reason God will send them strong *delusion*, that they should believe the lie." When we are deluded, it means that we have believed "the lie." This confirms what we saw previously in 1:25, they "exchanged the truth of God for the lie." Homosexuality is a

---

[134] See the *Ancient Commentary on Scripture (ACS) for Romans*, page 48.
[135] See Wiersbe's commentary on Romans 1:27.
[136] See the ACS by Origen and Pelagius, page 48.

lie. It is a delusion. I understand now why Joe Dallas, a former homosexual, entitled one of his books, *A Strong Delusion*.

It is difficult to understand why the "gay Christian" movement goes to this verse and explains away its meaning. What is there to misunderstand? Are any of these words positive? "Unnatural," "lust," "shameful," "penalty" (punishment), and "error" (delusion). The problem is not the proper biblical interpretation of a very clear text; the problem is that "men are burning in lust for other men." Gay Christians want this verse to say what will support their lifestyle. Unfortunately for them, God is against them.

A Debased Mind

"And even as they did not like to retain God in their knowledge, God gave them over to a debased mind, to do those things which are not fitting." (Romans 1:28)

The NLT and TLB translations read, respectively, "Since they thought it foolish to acknowledge God, He abandoned them to their foolish thinking and let them do things that should never be done" and "So it was that when they gave God up and would not even acknowledge Him, God gave them up to doing everything their evil minds could think of."

It is essential that we understand what the first part of this verse is saying. It does not say that they didn't know God or that God hid Himself from them. It was not a lack of knowledge. It was a deliberate ignorance. They knew the truth but suppressed it with their evil lifestyle. They knew the truth about God, but rejected it, and instead, they embraced the lie. Bruce writes, "These wrong ideas about God did not arise innocently; the knowledge of the true God was accessible, but men and women closed their minds to it." Edwards comments, "The problem is not lack of knowledge, but failure to acknowledge God and render proper worship and obedience." "They knew God" as verse 21 affirms, but they did not want God. That's why many translations use words like "they did not retain" nor "acknowledge" the truth of God, but rather, "they refused to think about God" or "keep Him in mind." They denied and dismissed Him. The living God clearly revealed Himself to them, but they rejected His revelation.

CHAPTER 4: *Vile Passions: Lesbians & Homosexuals*

The "futility of their thoughts" (v21) is now described as "a debased mind." God has given them over to this type of mind. This is now the third "God gave them over" statement. God gave them over to "uncleanness," "vile passions," and "a debased mind." Translators use varying words like "depraved mind," "corrupted mind," "useless mind," "worthless thinking," and "foolish thinking." The UBS translators say, "A mind that is completely twisted." The Greek word for "depraved" is "adokimos," which means "unapproved; rejected; worthless (literally or morally)." *It's a mind that's good for nothing.* Connor writes, "A reprobate mind is a mind hardened against truth and in rebellion against God. A mind that rejects the truth against itself is open to total depravity."

With a mind like this, they "do things that should never be done" (NLT). At "Gay Pride Parades" in San Francisco, they inflate giant penises (balloons); at bath houses, groups of men jump on top of each other, men with men, committing acts of unbridled lust; and in Bible days, hundreds of men, perhaps thousands, young and old, are pounding on Lot's door so they can enter and have sex with God's angels. *They want to commit homosexual acts with angels sent by God to destroy them because of their homosexual acts!* This is total blasphemy!

We could say more of the many things "that should never be done," but Paul warns us in Ephesians 5:11-12, "And have no fellowship with the unfruitful works of darkness, but rather expose them. For it is shameful even to speak of those things which are done by them in secret." Homosexual and lesbian lifestyles are corrupt, dark, and perverse. Go ahead and call us "homophobic," "gay-haters," and "unloving." *The ones who really love you are not those who agree with your lifestyle, but those who warn you of the coming judgment of God on such wickedness. We have become your enemies because we tell you the truth of God.* Yes, we are all sinners. Yes, Jesus loves us. But, yes, all sinners must repent of their sins, renounce their dark ways, and embrace the truth that is in Jesus Christ. The key word for this hour is found in Acts 17:30-31, "God overlooked people's ignorance about these things in earlier times, but now He commands everyone everywhere to repent of their sins and turn to Him. For He has set a day for judging the world with justice by the man He has appointed, and He proved to everyone who this is by raising Him from the dead" (NLT). Jesus is the Judge who will judge the living and the dead.

In Summary

God's wrath is being revealed from heaven against all ungodliness and unrighteousness of men. These men are suppressing the true knowledge of God by their wickedness. The Lord is going out of His way to make Himself known to all men – through the gospel, through creation, and through the work of the Holy Spirit. However, rather than accept God, rather than glorify and thank Him as the awesome God that He is, man rejects Him and chooses to worship the creation instead of the Creator. *They worship the god that they made rather than the God who made them.*

When we abandon God, He abandons us to our evil desires. We become vain, futile, and foolish. We become wise at being foolish. We trade in the incorruptible and take instead what is corruptible. Because of this action, God gives us up to the lusts of our hearts. These lusts ultimately manifest themselves through our bodies. The internal perversions become external acts of sexual immorality. We dishonor and disgrace our magnificent bodies by sexual acts of wickedness. Women lust after other women; men burn in lust after other men; both doing what is shameful and vile. This is clear evidence that we have "exchanged the truth of God for the lie." Homosexuality is a lie. It is against nature. It is unnatural.

The unmatched rise of perverted same-sex relationships in our day is undeniable proof that we have rejected God and His ways. Our immorality exposes our idolatry. Rather than worship God, we worship our own bodies. Rather than bring Him pleasure, we bring ourselves pleasure. We've been warned by the apostle that if we sow to the flesh, we will reap destruction. *God doesn't have to send an earthquake; He just needs to leave us to ourselves. Often times, it is not His intervention, but His lack of it, that leads to our demise.* Nevertheless, God chooses to intervene, because His lack of anger would reveal a lack of love. He is just and punishes what is evil.

CHAPTER 4: *Vile Passions: Lesbians & Homosexuals*

Let's pray: *Lord, as Christians, we repent. We repent of being lukewarm. We repent because we have remained silent. We repent because we have feared persecution and rejection. We repent because many of us have been sexually immoral. We have fornicated, viewed pornography, and committed adultery. We have accepted homosexuality as acceptable in Your sight. Forgive us and cleanse us from all unrighteousness. Save Your remnant from among the homosexual community. Thank You, Lord, for Your mercy and grace toward all of us. Amen.*

5

Paul on Homosexuality

"Do you not know that the unrighteous will not inherit the kingdom of God? Do not be deceived. Neither fornicators, nor idolaters, nor adulterers, nor homosexuals, nor sodomites will inherit the kingdom of God." (1 Corinthians 6:9-10)

I will never forget the young man. He told me that he was a Christian. He attended church services every Sunday; he was actively involved in ministry to people; he gave to various Christian causes; he was a very likeable young man with a good personality. *He also told me that homosexuality was completely acceptable in God's eyes.* In other words, he said, homosexuality was not a sin.

I wanted to probe his line of reasoning. How did he arrive at such a conclusion? What sort of teaching was he receiving from his church? What Bible verses was he using to support his claim? How did this young Christian settle it in his mind that homosexuality was good and wholesome?

I sat down with him one day and ask him some questions.

"Mike, is it okay with you if I ask you a few questions about your beliefs?"

"Sure. No problem," he answered.

"Mike, I want you to be free to answer my questions with no fear of condemnation or intimidation. I really want to know what you believe. It's important to have sound doctrine in your life as a Christian, because what you believe will determine how you live."

"I understand that. Thank you."

"Here is my first question – and the one that's the most important of all the questions I will ask you. Do you believe that Jesus Christ of Nazareth – the Lord Jesus Christ of the Bible – do you believe that He is the *only* way of salvation? In other words, can a person get to heaven without going through Him and His work on the cross? Is there salvation in any other man or religion or system of works? Can a person be saved apart from the Lord Jesus Christ?"

"No, Jesus is the way, the truth, and the life. He is the only way of salvation," Mike answered.

"Good, that's what I believe too."

Here's my next question: "Do you believe in an eternal hell? Do you believe that the wicked dead are cast into the fire of hell? Or do you believe that everyone goes to heaven? Are you a universalist; that is, do you believe everyone will be in the presence of God in the end?"

Mike said, "Yes, I believe there is a literal hell. I'm not a universalist. I don't believe everyone goes to heaven. Certainly, murderers and rapists, and people like Adolf Hitler and Charles Manson, will be in hell. If people do not repent of their sins and believe in Jesus Christ, they will go to hell."

"Thank you for that answer. That's what I believe."

"Okay, let's get a little closer to what I'm interested in talking about. Do you believe that when a man and a woman have sexual intercourse – two people who are not married – like a boyfriend and girlfriend; do you believe what the Bible calls 'fornication' is sin? Is it sinful in God's eyes for unmarried men and women to have sex?"

"Yes, that's a sin. To have sex before marriage is a sin in God's eyes. That's true."

"Okay, what about married people? What if a married woman – Christian or non-Christian – has sex with another man who is married or not? What the Bible calls adultery, is that a sin?

CHAPTER 5: *Paul on Homosexuality*

Or what if a married man has sex with his married secretary? Is that considered sinful in God's eyes?"

"Yes, that's definitely a sin. Adultery can break up a marriage. One of the Ten Commandments says, 'Thou shalt not commit adultery.' It was written in stone. It is clearly something that God does not accept. Adultery is condemned in the Bible."

"So, what you're telling me is that any type of sexual behavior between people who are not married to each other is sin, is that right? I'm assuming that pornography, incest, molestation, or rape are evil as well. These sins are clearly wrong. Is that what you believe?"

"Yes, if a twenty-five-year-old unmarried woman has sexual intercourse with a thirty-year-old married man, that is sin. And all those other things you mentioned like pornography and rape are surely wrong in God's eyes."

"So, Mike, do you believe that sex between two men – two homosexuals – or two lesbians is sin? I'm talking married or unmarried? Does God approve of this type of sexual behavior? Wouldn't two unmarried homosexuals having sex be considered fornication? You've agreed that fornication and adultery are wrong, but do you believe homosexuality is wrong?"

Mike answered, "I don't know."

He looked down at the ground for a moment. He thought about what to say next. I sat and listened.

"After that line of questions, I guess I'm a little confused," he said.

"Mike, you just finished telling me that fornication, molestation, pornography, and adultery are all wrong in God's eyes. These sexual acts or behaviors are sin. So homosexuality, which is clearly condemned in both the Old and New Testament, must also be sin. In fact, fornication, adultery, and homosexuality are often found in the same verse, sentence, or chapter. They are grouped together and condemned as sinful together."

I concluded, "When the Bible uses other words, words that in the original Greek text were clearly sexual terms, they also represent sexual immorality. Words like 'lewdness,' 'lasciviousness,' 'concupiscence,' or even 'uncleanness.' These also are sexual sins of lust and corruption. Just because we don't see the word, 'adultery,' doesn't mean it's not a sexual sin. Paul often listed 'homosexuality' along with other words that you just told me were sins. If Paul condemned fornication, adultery, and homosexuality, why did you only agree with two out of the three? I'm not trying to be mean to you, Mike, but could it be that you're more influenced by our secular culture than the apostle Paul? Are you in agreement with worldly thinking but not biblical thinking?"

I'm sad to say that I couldn't get him to see the illogical conclusion of his beliefs. He needed more time to think about it. I'm just glad that I was able to get him to think further about his position. I appreciated his honesty and I believe a seed was planted in his heart that will help him discern God's truth in the future.

The only person in the New Testament who spoke explicitly about homosexuality was the apostle Paul. He talked about it in three different books that he wrote. *And each time, Paul clearly said that homosexuality was sin. Never once did he accept homosexual behavior as God's will for any man's life.* Let's go to 1 Corinthians 6:9-11, 1 Timothy 1:9-11, and Romans 1:26-27 and see what the Holy Spirit inspired the apostle Paul to write.

Homosexuality – An Eternal Issue
1 Corinthians 6:9-11

Homosexuality is far more than a social issue in our present culture. Homosexuality is an eternal issue. If two lesbians are living two together and having sex; if two homosexual men are living together and having sex; if they die in that state, and they do not repent, then they will go to hell. They *will not* inherit the kingdom of God. As harsh as this may sound, it is the unvarnished truth: *Homosexual acts or behavior condemn a man's soul to an eternity without God.* That's deadly serious. This really is an urgent issue.

We know this is true because of what Paul wrote in 1 Corinthians 6:9-11. These are some of the most powerful verses in the Bible for our current immoral and decadent society. Let's examine carefully what the apostle said. It is a matter of life and death. It is the difference between heaven and hell.

CHAPTER 5: *Paul on Homosexuality*

Here is what the apostle wrote in verse 9: "Do you not know that the unrighteous will not inherit the kingdom of God? Do not be deceived. Neither fornicators, nor idolaters, nor adulterers, nor homosexuals, nor sodomites..." These words are so important that we need to break them down word by word.

Notice the first four words – "Do you not know." This is Paul's favorite phrase in 1 Corinthians. *"Do you not know* that you are the temple of God and that the Spirit of God dwells in you?" (3:16) *"Do you not know* that a little leaven leavens the whole lump?" (5:6) *"Do you not know* that the saints will judge the world?" (6:2) *"Do you not know* that we shall judge angels?" (6:3) *"Do you not know* that your bodies are members of Christ?" (6:15) *"Do you not know* that he who is joined to a harlot is one body with her?" (6:16) *"Do you not know* that your body is the temple of the Holy Spirit who is in you, whom you have from God, and you are not your own?" (6:19) *"Do you not know* that those who minister the holy things eat of the things of the temple, and those who serve at the altar partake of the offerings of the altar?" (9:13) *"Do you not know* that those who run in a race all run, but only one receives the prize?" (9:24)

He used that phrase six times in this 6th Chapter. There was a lot of spiritual ignorance in the believers of Corinth. Paul wrote in 1 Corinthians, "Brothers, I do not want you to be ignorant" and in 2 Corinthians, "For we do not want you to be ignorant, brothers."[137] He didn't want the Christian "brothers" ignorant. They were walking in darkness and Paul came to bring light; they were walking in confusion and Paul brought clarity.

How this is needed today! So many well-meaning Christians are buying into the corruption and defilement of the unsaved culture and accepting it as good. The prophets of God said, "My people are destroyed for a lack of knowledge," "Woe to those who call evil good, and good evil; who put darkness for light, and light for darkness; who put bitter for sweet, and sweet for bitter!" and "they have not distinguished between the holy and unholy, nor have they made known the difference between the

---

[137] See 1 Corinthians 12:1 and 2 Corinthians 1:8.

unclean and the clean."[138] How we desperately need this discernment in our day!

One of the best ways to measure the true effectiveness of a minister today is to see how many people he is turning away from sin. This is huge. The Lord of hosts, speaking through the prophet Malachi, said that the true Levitical priests were those who "turned many away from iniquity" and Ezekiel wrote that the true priests were "those who teach My people the difference between the holy and the unholy, and cause them to discern between the unclean and the clean."[139] Perhaps the main reason we have unbiblical beliefs on homosexuality that send mixed signals and give little discernment is because people are not preaching and teaching the truth on this subject directly from the Bible. If we have all love and no truth, we will believe a lie.

Paul continues in verse 9 with these words: "The unrighteous will not inherit the kingdom of God." Some translations say, "wicked," and others say, "evil people." Paul is saying that not everyone is going to heaven. There are some "unrighteous" and "wicked" people who will not inherit God's kingdom.[140] If they are not going to heaven, then they are going to hell. Unlike most funerals, where it appears that everyone goes to heaven, Paul states emphatically that many are going to be lost forever in the lake of fire.

In this verse and the next, Paul is going to list exactly who these "evil people" are. He's not just going to single out homosexuals; no, he's going to name other sexually immoral people and those who do various wicked acts.

Paul states in verse 9 that "...they will not inherit the kingdom of God" and he ends in verse 10 with "... they will not inherit the kingdom of God." As one writer says, "Wickedness has no future with God."[141] Paul wrote this way in Ephesians: "For this you know, that no fornicator, unclean person, nor

---

[138] See Hosea 4:6; Isaiah 5:20; and Ezekiel 22:26.
[139] See Malachi 2:6 and Ezekiel 44:23.
[140] This is another of the many verses throughout the Bible that war against universalism and the teachings of Rob Bell.
[141] *1 Corinthians*, Marion L. Soards, New International Biblical Commentary (NIBC), Hendrickson Publishers, Peabody, Massachusetts, page 124.

CHAPTER 5: *Paul on Homosexuality*

covetous man, who is an idolater, has any inheritance in the kingdom of Christ and God."[142] A "fornicator" – a sexually immoral man or woman – those who are having sex with their boyfriend or girlfriend have no inheritance in the kingdom. Paul adds in the next verse of Ephesians, "Let no one deceive you with empty words, for because of these things the wrath of God comes upon the sons of disobedience." Don't be deceived he says. If someone tells you otherwise, it's nothing but "empty words." The truth is that "God's wrath" comes upon such people for their "disobedience."

Notice what Paul writes in Galatians 5:19-21, "Now the works of the flesh are evident, which are: adultery, fornication, uncleanness, lewdness, idolatry, sorcery, hatred, contentions, jealousies, outbursts of wrath, selfish ambitions, dissensions, heresies, envy, murders, drunkenness, revelries, and the like; of which I tell you beforehand, just as I also told you in time past, that those who practice such things will not inherit the kingdom of God." The first four sins listed here are sexual sins. The sins of "fornication," "adultery," "uncleanness," and "lewdness" will send a person to hell. Paul said it "in time past," and he says it again: "Those who practice such things will not inherit the kingdom of God." Adulterers will go to hell if they don't repent.

Did not the apostle John write the same things in Revelation? "But the cowardly, unbelieving, abominable, murderers, *sexually immoral*, sorcerers, idolaters, and all liars shall have their part in the lake which burns with fire and brimstone, which is the second death" and "But outside are dogs and sorcerers and *sexually immoral* and murderers and idolaters, and whoever loves and practices a lie."[143] An old children's hymn says it this way: "There is a city bright; closed are its gates to sin; none that defiles, shall ever enter in."

Paul now uses a Greek imperative verb of command: "Do not be deceived!" Don't let anyone deceive you. Paul said this over and over in his letters – "Do not be deceived," "Do not be deceived," and "Let no one deceive you by any means."[144] The

---

[142] See Ephesians 5:5.
[143] See Revelation 21:8 and 22:15.
[144] See 1 Corinthians 15:33; Galatians 6:7; and 2 Thessalonians 2:3.

apostle James warned us, "Do not be deceived."[145] The apostle John said, "Let no one deceive you."[146] And, of course, the Master Himself commanded, "Take heed that you not be deceived" and "Take heed that no one deceives you."[147] "Many are going to come" in these last days and "deceive many." *Let NO ONE deceive you is the key word for this late hour.*

Even with these warnings, many gullible Christians are accepting the teachings of universalism (everyone gets saved) and the lifestyle of "gay Christians" (they are normal like everyone else). This is a lie. They are deceived. They will not inherit the kingdom of God. They are going to hell. Homosexuality is an eternal issue!

"The serpent deceived Eve by his craftiness" is part of Paul's writings to the Corinthians.[148] The Revelator said, "The serpent of old, called the Devil and Satan, who deceives the whole world," "Satan will go out to deceive the nations," and "the devil, who deceived them, was cast into the lake of fire and brimstone."[149] The deceiver gets thrown into the lake of fire along with all the deceived.

Now Paul is going to give us the list of the "unrighteous" who don't "inherit the kingdom of God." Here are the first five people – "Neither fornicators, nor idolaters, nor adulterers, nor homosexuals, nor sodomites." Four out of the first five are the sexually immoral.

Recalling the interview I had with the young man at the beginning of this chapter, we have here "fornicators," "adulterers," "homosexuals," and "sodomites" all in one verse. Everyone on this list is bad. Everyone is unrighteous. Everyone is wicked. They are all "evil people." If you say that fornication and adultery are wrong, then you need to say that homosexuality is wrong too. If fornicators and adulterers are unrighteous, then sodomites are unrighteous as well. We can't say, "I don't know." We do know. We are not ignorant. We are not deceived. Just because the secular culture accepts it doesn't mean that Christians

---

[145] See James 1:16.
[146] See 1 John 3:7.
[147] See Luke 21:8 and Matthew 24:4.
[148] See 2 Corinthians 11:3. Compare also with 1 Timothy 2:14.
[149] See Revelation 12:9, 20:8 and 20:10.

CHAPTER 5: *Paul on Homosexuality*

too have to accept it. Homosexuality is wrong, and homosexuals and sodomites will not inherit the kingdom of God.

"Fornicators" – Paul just finished talking about "fornicators" in the previous chapter. He wrote, "I wrote to you in my epistle not to keep company with fornicators" and "I have written to you not to keep company with anyone named a brother, who is a fornicator...not even to eat with such a person." He added that we are supposed to "judge those who are inside" (the church or Christian community) and "put away the wicked person from your midst."[150] God judges people outside (the unbelievers), but the church is supposed to judge people inside (the believers). If we don't, "a little leaven will leaven the whole lump of dough." It will spread.

I remember very vividly going to the house of a Christian woman who decided to move in with her unsaved boyfriend. They were having sex secretly and she was attending church services every Sunday. When I confronted her about the immoral situation she was living in, she simply said, "You are judging me. The whole church is judging me. I don't want to go to a place where I'm being judged." The truth is the Bible says, "Fornicators and adulterers God will judge."[151] The reason the church and its leaders must pronounce judgment is because God already has. We are only agreeing with God.

"Adulterers" – God judges adulterers. David paid a heavy price for his adultery with Bathsheba. God commanded us not to commit adultery in the Ten Commandments. Solomon said that whoever commits adultery "destroys his own soul." Jesus warned one of the churches in Revelation, "Indeed I will cast her into a sickbed, and those who commit adultery with her into great tribulation, unless they repent of their deeds." Divorce multiplies adultery in our society, for Jesus said, "Whoever divorces his wife and marries another commits adultery; and whoever marries her who is divorced from her husband commits adultery." You don't

---

[150] See 1 Corinthians 5:9-13.
[151] See Hebrews 13:4. The writer of Hebrews had already warned us to not be "a fornicator like Esau" in Hebrews 12:16. Esau sold himself out for "one morsel of food" or a "single meal." He lost it all for a bowl of stew. That's what fornicators do – they lose everything for a few minutes of sex.

have to commit the physical act; adultery can happen over and over again in the hearts of God's people – "But I say to you that whoever looks at a woman to lust for her has already committed adultery with her in his heart."[152] Among a long list of sins, Jesus said in Mark 7:21-23, "For from within, out of the heart of men, proceed evil thoughts, adulteries, fornications, lewdness, an evil eye...all these evil things come from within and defile a man." Adultery and fornication – along with many other sins – are evil and they defile (corrupt) a man.

"Homosexuals" – The Greek noun used here by Paul in 1 Corinthians 6:9 basically means "soft" or "soft ones." It was the word Jesus used when describing people who wore "soft garments" or "soft clothing."[153] The KJV accurately translates the word as "effeminate." The margin of my Bible gives an alternative translation as "a catamite," or by definition, "a young partner of a gay man; a boy kept by a man for sexual intercourse." One translation says, "Men who let other men use them for sex" and Warren Wiersbe says, "'Effeminate' and 'abusers' describe the passive and active partners in a homosexual relationship." Today, when two homosexuals marry, one of them is usually called "the wife" in the relationship," while the other is "the husband." The wife is the effeminate one. He is soft. He exhibits behavior normally associated with the feminine gender. They are men who act like women.

"Sodomites" – A "sodomite" was an "inhabitant of Sodom." Sodom was one of the wicked, homosexual-dominated, cities of Genesis 19 that God destroyed by fire and brimstone. The word, "homosexual," was only introduced in the English language in the 1890s. Prior to that time, the universal word used in English speaking countries for men who committed "anal intercourse" with other men was "sodomite."

The Greek word that Paul used here for "sodomite" is very interesting. It is the compound noun, "arsenokoites." "Arseno" is a Greek word for "male" and "koites" means "sexual intercourse." In fact, our English word for "coitus"[154] comes from

---

[152] See Proverbs 6:30; Revelation 2:22; Luke 16:18; and Matthew 5:28.
[153] See Matthew 11:8 (twice) and Luke 7:25.
[154] "Coitus" is defined in our English dictionaries as coming from Latin and means "sexual intercourse."

CHAPTER 5: *Paul on Homosexuality*

this word. Simply put, "arsenokoites" means "a man who has sexual intercourse with another man." Clearly, this is homosexual behavior. We will see this Greek word again shortly when we study 1 Timothy 1:10.

So, "homosexuals" (the effeminate; catamite) and "sodomites" (men who have sex with other men) are part of the unrighteous who will not inherit the kingdom of God. They are "corrupters of houses"[155] as one early church father called them. They will go to hell. Again, homosexuality is an eternal issue. "Do you not know?" Paul asks. Don't be deceived. Don't think it is acceptable in God's eyes.

Because it is not the subject of this chapter or this book, I'm not going to take much time to explain 1 Corinthians 6:10. But Paul gives us five other types of people who will not inherit the kingdom of God. They are "thieves, covetous, drunkards, revilers, and extortioners." There are many others besides the sexually immoral who are going to hell. Again, not everyone goes to heaven. Many will not inherit God's kingdom. As one commentator writes, "There is nothing inherently corrupt or corrupting in the kingdom of God: nor will anything of that nature be allowed to enter it. The two cannot mix."[156]

Well, the last few pages have been pretty rough. It seems like a lot of judgment, condemnation, and hell. Even though it is difficult, it is the truth. This is reality. It really does happen. Every day, tens of thousands of people go to hell. In our teachings on hell, we conservatively estimate that approximately 150,000 people go to hell every day! This is a frightening number. Proverbs 27:20 says, "Hell and Destruction are never full."

Let us now go to the redemptive part of Paul's teaching. There is hope. There is hope for all of us. There is hope for the homosexuals and sodomites. The Lord is not willing that any should perish, but that all come to repentance. God is commanding all men everywhere to repent because He has

---

[155] *Ancient Commentary on Scripture*, Ignatius of Antioch, New Testament, Volume VII, 1-2 Corinthians, Inter-Varsity Press, Downers Grove, Illinois, page 53.
[156] *The Message of 1 Corinthians*, David Prior, The Bible Speaks Today, Inter-Varsity Press, Downers Grove, Illinois, page 88.

appointed a day (the Day of the Lord) when He is going to judge all men by the Man He has appointed – Jesus Christ.[157]

Here is a great verse of hope and restoration. Verse 11 reads, "And that is what some of you were. But you were washed, you were sanctified, you were justified in the name of the Lord Jesus Christ and by the Spirit of our God." One translation says, "Some of you used to be like that. But now…" Some of you were homosexuals, sodomites, adulterers, and fornicators, BUT NOW. "But now" indicates a change. "But now" means that there was repentance. "But now" means that any of us can have a fresh start with Christ in our hearts. Jesus changes everything. The powerful truth that verse 11 teaches is that "homosexuality can be abandoned with God's help."[158] Many books have been written by ex-homosexuals attesting to the truth of these words. William Consiglio wrote a book entitled *Homosexual No More*.

There were three things that happened to us when we gave our hearts and lives to Jesus Christ. "But now you are washed, you are sanctified, and you are justified." These three things have happened "in the name of the Lord Jesus and by the Spirit of our God." The authority of Jesus Christ and the power of the Holy Spirit have made us whole. We are changed. We are different. We have been transformed. Hallelujah!

"You were washed" – the New Testament says a lot about being washed and cleansed by God. When Saul (apostle Paul) was persecuting the church terribly, the Lord knocked him down by His grace and saved him. He was told "Arise and be baptized, and *wash away your sins*, calling on the name of the Lord." Paul would later write that Jesus Christ "sanctifies and cleanses her (the church) with the *washing of water* by the word." The Word of God has the powerful effect of cleansing our hearts and souls from all defilement.

As Paul wrote here in verse 11, the Spirit of God is directly involved in our sanctification and cleansing. "According to His mercy He saved us, through the *washing* of regeneration

---

[157] See 2 Peter 3:9-10 and Acts 17:30-31.
[158] *1 Corinthians*, Craig Blomberg, The NIV Application Commentary, Zondervan Publishing House, Grand Rapids, Michigan, page 124.

CHAPTER 5: *Paul on Homosexuality*

and renewing of the Holy Spirit." There is a washing. There is a regeneration and renewing. All of this is by the Holy Spirit.

The apostle John, while writing on the island of Patmos, reminds us in Revelation 1:5-6: "To Him who loved us and *washed us from our sins* in His own blood, and has made us kings and priests to His God and Father, to Him be glory and dominion forever and ever! Amen!" Yes, it is by the precious blood of Christ that we have been washed. Later, John would write, "These are the ones who have *washed their robes* and made them white in the blood of the Lamb." What was once black is now made white by the blood. The apostle had also written in 1 John 1:7, 9, "The blood of Jesus Christ His Son *cleanses* us from all sin" and "If we confess our sins, He is faithful and just to forgive us our sins and to *cleanse* us from all unrighteousness." We are washed and cleansed by the blood of Jesus Christ!

For the homosexual or sodomite – you can be washed. You can be made whole, new, clean, and well. Don't reject the One who is drawing and convicting you. Draw near to Jesus in full assurance and faith by His blood. Jesus died on the cross so you could be made whole – spirit, soul, and body. If Saul could be forgiven as a "blasphemer" and a murderer, then surely you can be forgiven of your homosexual acts. No sin is too vile that the blood of Jesus cannot cover.

"You were sanctified" – the high calling of God in Christ Jesus for *every* believer is that he must be holy. God has set us apart and consecrated us for His purpose and His will. Every true Christian embraces the command of 1 Peter 1:16: "Be holy, for I am holy." If we don't walk in this holiness, we will not "see the Lord" nor will we be "useful for the Master."[159] The Lord cannot use an unclean vessel.

What amazes me is how the Lord has gone out of His way to make sure we are sanctified. It is all because of Him. You can't be holy without divine help. In 1 Thessalonians, a book that shows us how to be ready for His coming, Paul commands Christians to be "blameless in holiness."[160] He assures that this incredible state of being is possible because "the God of peace

---

[159] See Hebrews 12:14 and 2 Timothy 2:21.
[160] See 1 Thessalonians 3:13.

Himself will sanctify you completely; and may your whole spirit, soul, and body be preserved blameless at the coming of our Lord Jesus Christ."[161] God wants to "sanctify you completely!" He wants us to be holy as He is holy.

Notice how the Lord sanctifies the believer: "Sanctify them through the truth," "sanctified by faith in Me," "sanctified by the Holy Spirit," "sanctified in Christ Jesus," "sanctified by the Word," "sanctified by Christ's offering on the cross," and "sanctified by His own blood."[162] This is all the work of God! His truth, His faith, His Spirit, His Word, His offering, and His own blood – Only in Him, through Him, and by Him can you be holy in His presence. You were sanctified! It was "in the name of the Lord Jesus and by the Spirit of God."

What does this have to do with a homosexual? Everything. He can be washed, cleansed, and sanctified. He can be thoroughly purged by God's grace. The slate can be wiped completely clean. The mind can be renewed and transformed. The homosexual can be totally and wholly delivered from his former lifestyle and given a new heart and new mind. The old has passed; the new has come!

For all of us – including the homosexual – our only hope is in Jesus Christ the Lord. Nothing else can change us. Nothing else works. And, in the end, eternal salvation is at stake. Everything that we need for godliness is found in Jesus.

"You were justified" – the Greek word here for "justified" is a legal term that means "to be rendered or declared just or innocent." In a court of law, when the judge or jury states, "Not guilty," that means you are cleared. You can go free. You were found innocent. All the charges against you were dropped.

In the heavenly court, the only One who can justify you is God. It was through the death, burial and resurrection of Jesus Christ that anyone is justified in God's eyes.

This is the powerful message of the Book of Romans – "We have been justified by His grace through His blood." We are declared innocent with the innocence of Christ. He paid the price.

---

[161] See 1 Thessalonians 5:23.
[162] See John 17:17, 17:19; Acts 26:18; Romans 15:16; 1 Corinthians 1:2; Ephesians 5:26; 1 Timothy 4:5; Hebrews 10:10 and 13:12.

CHAPTER 5: *Paul on Homosexuality*

He took the "death penalty" for our guilt. The Innocent One was punished while the guilty ones were set free. This is the exchange that took place on the cross. Believers are justified by our faith in Him and imputed with His perfect righteousness. We are right in God's eyes because of Jesus and His grace – that's justification.

What do the Scriptures say? How are we justified? "Having been *justified* by faith," "that we might be *justified* by faith," "knowing that a man is not *justified* by the works of the law but by faith in Jesus Christ," "by Him everyone who believes is *justified* from all things from which you could not be *justified* by the law of Moses," "being *justified* freely by His grace through the redemption that is in Christ Jesus," "having been *justified* by His grace we should become heirs according to the hope of eternal life," and "having now been *justified* by His blood."[163] The Bible says you are justified "by faith, by His grace, and by His blood."

The bottom-line is that God has cleared us of all charges against us. Romans 8:33-34 say, "Who shall bring a charge against God's elect? It is God who justifies. Who is he who condemns? It is Christ who died, and furthermore is also risen, who is even at the right hand of God, who also makes intercession for us." God justifies because Christ died. Who has a charge against us? Who can condemn us? The Ultimate Judge has declared us innocent! You were justified!

This is great news for all sinners. This is great news for me. This is great news for the homosexual or lesbian. No matter how many "encounters" a homosexual has had, he can be "cleared of all charges" by the blood of Jesus Christ. By faith in His grace, the homosexual has been freed from his past. Who can condemn him when Christ has justified Him. This is the gospel. Jesus Christ has made a way for us to stand innocent and righteous in God's eyes. "Now to Him who is able to keep you from falling and to present you before His glorious presence without fault and with great joy!"[164]

---

[163] See Romans 5:1; Galatians 3:24; Galatians 2:16; Acts 13:39; Romans 3:24; Titus 3:7; Romans 5:9.
[164] See Jude 1:24.

I want to conclude this discussion on 1 Corinthians 6:9-11 with a conversation that I had with a young Christian youth leader that I met recently. She was troubled by how many teenagers in her church's youth group are okay with homosexuality. Homosexuality to them is normal. There's nothing wrong with it. Nearly everyone at their schools – principal, teachers, parents, and students – have accepted the homosexual and lesbian lifestyle. These teens have been run over by the LGBTQ agenda. Gay marriage is now the law of the land. Why fight it? Let's move on, they say.

"What can I tell these teenagers?" she asked. "It seems that nothing I say makes a difference. Everyone has accepted it. It appears that I'm the only one who is strange; everyone else is normal. What do I do?"

These are great questions. This is the new reality that Christians are facing here in America and around the world. We are calling homosexuality "evil"; the world is calling it "good." When the dust clears, this is the real issue.

Where do we begin so that young Christians can see that homosexuality is evil?

Based on what we've discussed in this chapter, let me offer this advice: *Make it an eternal issue.* Homosexuality is an eternal issue. It is either heaven or hell. What counts is not what other teens or the school say about homosexuality; what really counts is what God will say on Judgment Day.

So, if homosexuality is sin – and it is sin – who is the one that really loves the homosexual? Is it the people who tell the lesbians and homosexuals that everything is fine with them? Or is it the ones who speak the truth in love and are doing everything to ensure that they don't go to hell? I believe it is the true believers – who declare the truth of God in love to homosexuals – that really love them. The others are merely encouraging them toward their destruction. When we all stand before God, which of us will have blood on our hands?

Are the words of the prophet Ezekiel not appropriate here? "When I say to the wicked, 'You shall surely die,' and you give him no warning, nor speak to warn the wicked from his wicked way, to save his life, that same wicked man shall die in his iniquity; but his blood I will require at your hand. Yet, if you warn the wicked, and he does not turn from his wickedness, nor from his wicked way, he shall die in his iniquity; but you have delivered your soul."[165] We need to be cleared of the blood of others. We do this by declaring to them "the whole counsel of God." Here from Ezekiel's words, we learn that *we need to speak what God is speaking*. Again, maybe that's the problem: Too many Christians don't know what God is saying about homosexuality. That's why I wrote this book.

Homosexuality is Against All Sound Teaching
1 Timothy 1:9-11

In 1 Corinthians 6:9, Paul used the word, "sodomite." He wrote that "sodomites" would not inherit the kingdom of God. As you recall, the Greek word that Paul used was "arsenokoites," a compound word that literally means "a male who has sexual intercourse with another man." It is another word for "homosexual." "Arsenokoites" are "homosexuals."

Paul uses "arsenokoites" again here in 1 Timothy 1:10 and it is variously translated as "sodomites," "perverts," "people who practice homosexuality," and "those who have sexual relations with those of the same sex." Clearly, Paul is speaking here about homosexuality. Why did Paul bring up homosexuality in this verse? Let's look closely.

1 Timothy 1:9 reads, "Knowing this: that the law is not made for a righteous person, but for the lawless and insubordinate, for the ungodly and for sinners, for the unholy and profane, for murderers of fathers and murderers of mothers, for manslayers." The New Living Translation (NLT) says, "For the law was not intended for people who do what is right. It is for people who are lawless and rebellious, who are ungodly and sinful, who consider nothing sacred and defile what is holy, who kill their father or mother or commit other murders." Why does Paul bring up "the law," and why was it important to the context?

Both 1 Timothy and 2 Timothy are written by Paul to address all the false teachers and false doctrines that Timothy was facing in the city of Ephesus. The Chapter heading of one

---

[165] See Ezekiel 3:18-19.

commentary says, "The Charge to Timothy Concerning False Teachers."[166] Another called it: "The Charge: Stop the False Teachers."[167] Paul writes, "I left you in Ephesus that you may command some that they teach no other doctrine." False teachers were teaching "fables," "endless genealogies," "old wives' fables," "useless wranglings," "that gain is godliness," and "that the resurrection had already past." These were evil men like "Phygellus and Hermogenes," "Hymenaeus and Philetus," and "Alexander the coppersmith." They were "evil men and imposters who grow worse and worse, deceiving and being deceived." Paul warned that gullible believers were "heaping up for themselves teachers" to scratch their "itching ears" and were "turning their ears away from the truth and turning aside to fables." Paul told Timothy that "the Spirit clearly says that in latter times some will depart from the faith, giving heed to deceiving spirits and doctrines of demons."

There were so many false teachers and false doctrines that Paul had to teach "sound doctrine" or "good doctrine," and Timothy had to "carefully follow my doctrine." Because "doctrine" was so important, Paul told him, "Till I come, give attention to reading, to exhortation, to *doctrine*," "Take heed to yourself and to the *doctrine*," honor elders, "especially those who labor in the word and *doctrine*," and preach "the *doctrine* which accords with godliness." His anchor had to be "All Scripture which is given by inspiration of God and is profitable for *doctrine*." That's why 1 Timothy and 2 Timothy are part of the "Pastoral Epistles" to train ministers on how to maintain sound doctrine and guard the flock against false teachings.

Rather than preaching "godly edification," "love from a pure heart," and "sincere faith," some people, "having strayed, have turned aside to idle talk, desiring to be teachers of the law, understanding neither what they say nor the things which they affirm" (1:6-7). Paul actually says that "the law is good if one uses it lawfully" (1:8). In other words, the law of God (of Moses)

---

[166] *First Timothy*, D. Edmond Hiebert, Everyman's Commentary, Moody Press, Chicago, Illinois, page 27.
[167] *1 and 2 Timothy, Titus*, Gordon D. Fee, New International Biblical Commentary, Hendrickson Publishers, Peabody, Massachusetts, page 39.

CHAPTER 5: *Paul on Homosexuality*

can have a good purpose. It gives insight for living. It gives instruction in righteousness. It gives the knowledge of sin.[168] God's law is the truth and reveals the mind and will of the Lord. There is nothing wrong with the law.

However, it's the *application* of the law that was in question. Who was it for? Well, Paul says that it was NOT *for* a righteous man. "The law has little relevance for law-abiding people."[169] It was for wicked and rebellious people. As Christians, we don't live under the law; we live under the grace of God. The works of the law don't save us; faith in Jesus Christ saves us as Galatians, Chapter 3 so confidently affirms.

That is the background to 1 Timothy 1:9-11.

Paul starts by writing, "Knowing this: that the law was not made for a righteous person." That's not who it is for. Rather, it is for ungodly people. Paul then writes to identify who they are in verses 9-10. He starts with four pairs of people grouped together. Let's briefly state who are the wicked people:

"Lawless and insubordinate" – By definition, lawless people are those who are out of control and disorderly. They are troublemakers. One translation calls them "lawbreakers." They play the game of life with "no rules," and they do whatever they want.

The "insubordinate" are people who refuse to obey orders or submit to authority. Literally, the Greek word is people who are "unsubdued." You cannot bring them under control. They are rebels and rebellious. One translation says, "Those who are against the law and refuse to follow it." I recently watched in dismay a series of documentaries by *National Geographic* (Lockdown) on some of the worst prisons (and prisoners) here in America. Some men were so wild and belligerent that six or seven prison officers had to tackle these men, handcuff them, and tie them up. These are like the rebellious people that Paul speaks of here.

---

[168] See Romans 2:17-24, 3:20, and 7:7-12.
[169] *The Pastoral Epistles*, Donald Guthrie, Revised Edition, Tyndale New Testament Commentaries, Eerdmans Publishing Company, Grand Rapids, Michigan, page 71.

"Ungodly and sinners" – Ungodly means people who are irreverent toward God. They are "unlike God." These are people who live as if there is no God. They do everything to intentionally violate God's moral laws. "Sinners" are simply those who continue to live their own "sinful ways."

"Unholy and profane" – There are people who live right and keep themselves pure and free of defilement. The "unholy" are the exact opposite. They defile themselves with a wicked lifestyle. They indulge in worldly things and corrupt their hearts with evil behavior. They trample underfoot the sacred things of God. "Profane" literally means "to cross a threshold." They are people who "cross the line." When someone starts to have sex with a minor, they have crossed the line. Hebrews 12:16 calls "Esau" a "profane person." He sold his very valuable birthright for a "single morsel of food." When an unmarried young man and young woman have sex for the first time and lose their virginity, they sacrifice what is sacred for what is vile all in about five to ten minutes. They sacrifice their future on the altar of the immediate. What a terrible price to pay.

"Murderers of fathers and murderers of mothers" – God commanded us to honor our father and mother; here are people who are killing them. The law of God had some very harsh things to say about anyone who mistreated his father or mother. Exodus 21:17 says, "He who curses his father or his mother shall surely be put to death" and Deuteronomy 27:16 reads, "Cursed is the one who treats his father or his mother with contempt." If this is what happens to those who curse their father and mother, what will happen to those who murder them?!

I saw a documentary recently of a rich, seventeen-year-old girl who put a kitchen knife through one of her mom's eye sockets in a moment of rage because her mom opposed the premarital sex she was having with her twenty-one-year-old boyfriend. The boyfriend helped to kill the girl's mother. One Greek dictionary defines the word for "murderer of mothers" as "a mother-thresher." It gives the idea of tearing someone apart. You want them torn to pieces.

"Manslayers" – Ever since Cain murdered Abel in Genesis 4, we have been killing each other on planet earth. The

Bible documents many murders. God commanded us, "Thou shalt not kill," but that hasn't stopped us.

Year by year, Brazil has the highest number of murders of any country in the world. Recently, 55,574 people were killed there in one year or about 152 each day. That's a lot of death. A "manslayer" is a person who kills men. Our prisons are filled with "manslayers."

Before we go to 1 Timothy 1:10, what can we learn of the list of people in verse 9? What stands out as you read this list? *They are all evil people.* Someone who can murder his mother is a wicked person. Anyone can draw that conclusion. This is a critical point as we move into verse 10.

"For fornicators, for sodomites, for kidnappers, for liars, for perjurers, and if there is any other thing that is contrary to sound doctrine." To the terrible list of verse 9, Paul adds five more people.

"Fornicators" – The Greek word is "pornos." It is the exact same Greek noun that Paul used in 1 Corinthians 6:9. Some translations call them the "sexually immoral," "sexual perverts," or "whoremongers." They are people who give themselves over to sexual sins. They come under God's judgment (Hebrews 13:4) and they will not inherit the kingdom of God (Ephesians 5:5). "Esau" was considered a "fornicator" in Hebrews 12:16.

"Sodomites" – Not much needs to be said. It is "arsenokoites" or "those men who have sexual intercourse with other men." These are the homosexuals. They are included with a list of very evil people like "murderers" and "kidnappers." Kidnappers are next.

"Kidnappers" – Some translations use "slave traders" or "those who sell slaves." The old KJV had the intense, "menstealers." The Greek compound word means literally "someone who brings men to his feet." Strong's dictionary calls him, "an enslaver." The law of God said, "Anyone who kidnaps another and either sells him or still has him when he is caught must be put to death" and "If a man is caught kidnapping one of his brother Israelites and treats him as a slave or sells him, the kidnapper must die. You must purge the evil from among you."[170]

---

[170] See Exodus 21:16; Deuteronomy 24:7.

"Liars" – Jesus said that the devil "is a liar and the father of lies." Paul agreed that "Cretans are always liars." The ultimate "liar" was "he who denies that Jesus is the Christ."[171] God hates lying so much that Revelation 21:8 says, "All liars shall have their part in the lake which burns with fire and brimstone."

Finally, "Perjurers" – One translation has "those who don't tell the truth under oath." This is the only time it is mentioned in the New Testament, so other verses can't help us. In a court of law, we have to raise our right hand and swear to tell the truth. Those who lie to the court commit perjury. The Latin word, "perjurare," means to "swear falsely." We swore to tell the truth but we told a lie instead.

Paul could have made the list longer, but he concludes, "...and if there is any other thing that is contrary to sound doctrine." He made a similar statement in Galatians 5:21, after his list of the works of the flesh – "and other sins like these." Thus, Paul only gave us a limited list of people, not an exhaustive one.

This list in 1 Timothy 1:9-10 does not include "sins," but "sinners." He said, "murderers," not "murder"; "kidnappers," not "kidnapping"; "fornicators," not "fornication." He also listed "sodomites," not "sodomy." He's talking about people.

Let's get to the subject at hand. "Sodomites" – those who live as homosexuals – are contrary to all sound doctrine and teaching. It is totally contrary "to the glorious gospel of the blessed God which was committed to my trust" (1:11). How can any Christian who takes God's Word seriously conclude that homosexuality is good? Homosexuals are doing evil things. They are listed along with the "lawless," "rebellious," "ungodly," "unholy," "profane," "murderers of fathers," "murderers of mothers," "manslayers," "fornicators," "kidnappers," "liars," and "perjurers."

Once again, going back to the interview with the young man, he says that "fornication" is wrong, but about "homosexuality," "I don't know." In this verse, just like 1 Corinthians 6:9, "sodomites" are listed right next to "fornicators." If one is wrong, so is the other.

---

[171] See John 8:44; Titus 1:12; and 1 John 2:22.

CHAPTER 5: *Paul on Homosexuality*

Homosexuality is Lust & Unnatural
Romans 1:26-27

This is the third place in the New Testament where Paul wrote about homosexuality.

He speaks specifically about lesbians and homosexuals. We covered Romans 1:18-28 almost word for word in a previous written teaching,[172] so I will only give a summary of verses 26 and 27 in this section.

Let's start with the "lesbian verse." This is the only verse in the entire Bible that speaks directly about lesbianism. Romans 1:26 reads, "For this reason God gave them up to vile passions. For even their women exchanged the natural use for what is against nature."

When people reject their Creator, God gives them over to the "lusts of their hearts" and they begin to "dishonor their bodies among themselves" (1:24). This is an act of "uncleanness." What begins in the heart is acted out in the body. That's what lesbianism and homosexuality are about – lusts and corrupt sex.

Paul writes, "For this reason." It is because women have *exchanged* the "glory of God" for the "corrupt image of man," and because they *exchanged* "the truth of God" for "the lie of man," that women have *exchanged* what was "natural" for what is "unnatural." This exchange is the massive confusion we have today with people's sexuality.

Lesbianism is "against nature." The great "Creator" of verse 25 did not create "the creature" this way. God created women to have a natural relationship with a man. When women get together with other women sexually, it is a "vile passion." It is a "shameful lust" or "evil desire." God gives these lesbians over to this wicked passion because they have rejected Him.

In Romans 1:27, the men do what the women have done. "Likewise also the men, leaving the natural use of the woman, burned in their lust for one another, men with men committing what is shameful, and receiving in themselves the penalty of their error which was due." Another translation reads, "In the same

---

[172] See Chapter 4, *Vile Passions – Lesbians & Homosexuals*, or at www.teacherofthebible.com.

way the men also abandoned natural relations with women and were inflamed with lust for one another. Men committed indecent acts with other men, and received in themselves the due penalty for their perversion."

The men also begin to do what is "unnatural." God created a man to be with a woman in marital love and faithfulness. Instead, they are "burning" or "inflamed in lust" for another man. When men lust after other men, they do what is "shameful" and "indecent." They will then receive a "penalty" for their "perversion."

In three verses – Romans 1:24, 1:26, and 1:28 – Paul says that God has "given over" or "abandoned" these lesbians and homosexuals to "uncleanness," "vile passions," and a "depraved mind." God created man in His image, but because his "thoughts became futile," instead of being "wise," he became a "fool." This "depraved" or "debased" mind began to think corrupt thoughts. This is why they began to do what "is not right" or "not fitting." Rather than embrace the truth of who God is, they rejected it. They "suppressed the truth in unrighteousness." Their "ungodliness and unrighteousness" provoked God's "wrath." "The wrath of God was revealed" when He gave them over to what they wanted. There are always tragic results when God gives us what we want. The psalmist said in Psalm 106:15, "So God gave them what they asked for, but sent a wasting disease upon them." Why did this happen? "Because they (the Israelites) lusted exceedingly in the wilderness" (106:14).

If you want to see how far men and women have moved away from God's original design; if you want to see how far we have veered from God's truth; if you want to see how "against nature" we have become; then just look at lesbianism and homosexuality. They are not necessarily worse than other sins; they simply illustrate best how "the creature" has rejected "the Creator" and done what is "against nature."

No one with any honesty and integrity can read these verses in Romans 1:26-27 and conclude that God approves of homosexual behavior. In a very overwhelming and convincing way, Paul clearly teaches why such a lifestyle is corrupt and shameful. Rather than endorsing such lustful acts, Paul says they bring "the judgment of God" and the "wrath of God." No one ever

CHAPTER 5: *Paul on Homosexuality*

has to say, "I don't know," regarding what God says about homosexuality. Moses wrote, "Men, you must not have sexual relations with another man as with a woman. That is a terrible sin!" or "Do not practice homosexuality, having sex with another man as with a woman. It is a detestable sin."[173] Homosexuality is an abomination in the eyes of the Lord.

In Summary

In 1 Corinthians 6:9-11, the apostle Paul taught us that "homosexuals" and "sodomites" are part of the "unrighteous" who "will not inherit the kingdom of God." These men are listed along with "fornicators" and "adulterers" because these are the sexually immoral that we are not "to keep company with" nor "even eat with such persons" (5:9-13). They are to be judged and expelled from the Christian community so that "a little yeast doesn't spread through the whole batch of dough" (5:6).

Instead of living in homosexuality – or any other sin – you can be "washed," "sanctified," and "justified" by the Lord Jesus Christ and the Holy Spirit of God. There is always redemption, salvation, and deliverance for those who repent and turn to God.

In 1 Timothy 1:9-11, Paul makes it clear that the "arsenokoites" – those men who have sexual relations with other men – are doing what is "against sound doctrine." Homosexuality is not "according to the glorious gospel of the blessed God." No, it is listed right along with "fornicators" as one of the sexually immoral. The "sodomites" are listed along with the lawless, rebellious, unholy, ungodly, profane, murderers, kidnappers, liars, and perjurers. Everyone on this list does what is evil and wicked. If a "fornicator" is condemned before God, so must a "sodomite" be.

Finally, in Romans 1:26-27, we see that "lesbians" are engaged in "vile passions" which are "unnatural." Homosexuals are not "in love," but "burning in lust for one another." They do what is "shameful" and "disgraceful." From the beginning, "the Creator" created "the creature" to "worship Him" and be "thankful." Instead, both men and women have rejected the true

---

[173] See the ERV and NLT translations of Leviticus 18:22.

revelation of the glorious and holy God, so He has given them over to the "lusts of their hearts" to eventually "dishonor their bodies among themselves."

6

A Christian Manifesto on Homosexuality

> *"If a man practices homosexuality, having sex with another man as with a woman, both men have committed a detestable act. They must be put to death; their blood will be on their own heads.*
> *(Leviticus 20:13)*

Because of the rise of homosexuality in our city, state, nation, and world, we, the people of Clovis Christian Center, are making a public declaration of our beliefs on homosexuality. Because the Bible, God's Holy Word, is our final authority on all matters of belief, doctrine, godliness, life, revelation, and truth, then we accept its clear instruction on the subject of homosexuality as the Lord's revealed will for all of mankind (not just Christians).

This is a manifesto. "Manifesto" is a Latin word that basically means "make evident." It is a public, written declaration of one's beliefs, principles, and objectives.

Because of the teachings of the Bible, we have written a twenty-one-point manifesto on what we believe about homosexuality. Let us start with the critical issue of marriage.

Regarding Marriage & Gay Marriages

We will always affirm and never shrink back from declaring that the only marriage that is acceptable in the sight of God is that between one man and one woman.[174]

From the very beginning, in the earliest chapters of Genesis, God stated that a woman (female) was taken out of man (male), and the man (male) was to leave his father (male) and mother (female) and be united to his wife (female). The prophet Malachi reminds us that a man's wife is "his partner" and she is "the wife of your marriage covenant."

Jesus Himself quoted from Genesis and said that "God made them male and female." He added that a man must be united to his wife and leave his father and mother. They were no longer two, but one, and what God had joined together, man was not to separate.

The apostle Paul stated plainly that a "married woman is bound to her husband as long as he is alive." And it was only after he died that she was released from the law of marriage and could marry another man. Paul would add in 1 Corinthians that "a man should have his own wife, and each woman her own husband."

Paul reminds us that ultimately marriage reveals the relationship between Christ (husband) and His church (bride). The church is always portrayed as a "she," "her," "wife," or "bride." Anything different is a perversion. A man must love his wife like Christ loved the church. The wife was to respect and submit to her husband. He would later tell the Colossian church that "husbands are to love their wives and not be harsh against them, and wives are to submit to their husbands as it is fitting in the Lord."

---

[174] See Genesis 2:24; Malachi 2:14; Mark 10:6-9; Romans 7:2-3; 1 Corinthians 7:2; Ephesians 5:22-33; Colossians 3:18-19; 1 Timothy 3:2; and 1 Peter 3:1-7.

CHAPTER 6: *A Christian Manifesto on Homosexuality*

Leaders in the church (bishops, overseers) were to be the "husband of but one wife."

We know that the apostle Peter was married to a woman. Jesus healed Peter's mother-in-law of a fever, and later on, Paul would write that Peter brought a "believing wife with him" whenever he traveled.[175] Peter wrote about husband (male) and wife (female) relationships in his first letter, and he illustrated proper marriage relationships by using "Abraham and Sarah" as an example. His language clearly reveals that marriage is between a man and a woman.

I know that all of the above verses are well-known to Bible-believing Christians, but let us state a fundamental truth right now: *There is not a single verse in the entire Bible that endorses or supports marriage between a man and a man or a woman and a woman. In fact, whenever the Bible mentions such relationships, it clearly speaks against them!*

We wholeheartedly agree and align ourselves completely with the Lord Jesus, Moses the lawgiver, and the Apostle Paul, that a man (male) shall leave his father (male) and mother (female), and shall be joined to his wife (female), and these two shall become one flesh.[176]

A father is a male. A mother is a female. Thus, a man and a woman come together in marriage, bear children, raise a family, and these children eventually leave their parents and start their own family. This simple, God-ordained plan for families was endorsed by Moses, Jesus, and the apostle Paul. Jesus and Paul only affirmed what was already written "from the beginning." Nothing has changed. Thousands of years later, true Christian believers are still defending these original beliefs. We are commanded to "honor our father and mother," not our "two mothers" or "two fathers."

In our day and age, we have such confusing statements as a "woman marries her wife" or a "man lives with his husband." By its very definition in any good dictionary, a husband is "a man whom a woman marries" and a wife is "a woman whom a man

---

[175] See 1 Corinthians 9:5. He is called "Cephas" in this verse.
[176] See Genesis 2:24; Matthew 19:4-6; Mark 10:6-9; and Ephesians 5:31.

marries." The language of homosexual marriages is so bewildering that it even defies the rules of grammar and the established definition of words.

We believe that God's original purpose and design for mankind was that a man would marry a woman, bear children, raise a family, and thus fulfilled the biblical mandate to "be fruitful and multiply." This cannot be done by homosexual or lesbian couples on their own.[177]

Two homosexual men cannot produce a child and neither can two lesbian women. This fact supports Paul's assertion that these homosexual relationships are "unnatural" or "against nature." God commanded male and female species to board the ark so that they could continue to propagate on this earth. The "pairs" were not "male and male," but "male and female."

The command to "be fruitful and multiply" was evidence of God's "blessing." God blessed them in order to multiply. The Lord did this at the time of Adam and Eve when the human race began, and again at the time of Noah when the human race was "restarted." God told Noah that while others were killing each other and taking life, they were to "be fruitful and multiply."

The whole purpose of "two becoming one flesh" was for sexual intercourse and procreation. Thus, Malachi explains that the reason He made them one was because the Lord was "seeking godly offspring." The barren relationships of homosexual men cannot produce godly children.

Paul commanded "younger widows (women) to marry, to have children, and manage their homes." These women were to reject "sensual desires."

We believe that God desires for both the man and the woman to be virgins at the time of marriage, and if a man and a woman want to have sexual intercourse, then they must get married. And if they are Christians, they can only marry another Christian believer of the opposite sex.[178]

---

[177] See Genesis 1:28, 9:1, 9:7; Malachi 2:14-16; and 1 Timothy 5:14.
[178] 1 Corinthians 7:2, 7:25, 7:28, 7:37; Luke 1:27; Genesis 24:16; Leviticus 21:14; and 1 Corinthians 7:39.

CHAPTER 6: *A Christian Manifesto on Homosexuality*

Everywhere we turn today, unmarried men and women are having sexual intercourse without the commitment of marriage. The Bible calls this fornication. This is a great tragedy. Sex is a privilege reserved for married couples only.

The Old Testament priests were allowed to marry virgin girls only – they could not be divorced, widowed, or have previous sexual relationships (including living as a harlot). Rebekah, Isaac's future wife was described as "very beautiful, a virgin, no man had ever lain with her."[179]

The Lord placed a vaginal membrane called a hymen at the opening of a woman's vagina. This small membrane is filled with blood. When a man goes into his wife on wedded night, the hymen is broken, blood is shed, and that couple enter into a blood covenant meant to last forever.[180] Fathers must help their virgin sons and daughters protect their virginity. To fornicate is a great sin against the Lord. It is better to marry than to burn with passion. If two young people (male and female) cannot restrain themselves, and it is God's will for them to be married, and they genuinely love one another, then it is best to get married so they can have sex and not fornicate.

Paul commanded the "unmarried woman or virgin" to make it her aim or goal to be "holy (devoted) to the Lord in both body and spirit." Previously, he wrote that "the body is not meant for sexual immorality, but for the Lord, and the Lord for the body." We are to "flee sexual immorality." There are some sins that are so dangerous and deadly that the only recourse is to run from them! Joseph was very brave and bold when he fled from Potiphar's wife. When she tempted him to commit adultery with her, he told her this act would be a great sin against the Lord and then he ran out of the house. He was a man of strong character.

I thank God for the Virgin Mary. She set an example for all future women. Young ladies must keep themselves pure and reserve their virgin bodies for their future husband alone. Don't defile yourself with guys who are just lusting after your body. What a great difference between love and lust.

---

[179] See Genesis 24:16.
[180] See Deuteronomy 22:13-21.

Another great sin among Christians today is those who marry unbelievers. To marry an unbeliever is a direct act of disobedience against the Lord. Paul gave us the straight word on this matter: "Do not be yoked together with unbelievers. For what do righteousness and wickedness have in common? Or what fellowship can light have with darkness? What harmony is there between Christ and Belial (Satan)? What does a believer have in common with an unbeliever?"[181] We have nothing in common with unbelievers. We have no harmony with them. There can be no fellowship with the "dark side." Why would you want to marry someone who is serving the world, the flesh and the devil? Your marriage will be filled with trouble and confusion. The truth is that we are called to "be separate" and not to even "touch the unclean thing." Marrying an unbeliever totally compromises our relationship with Father God.

Because of the above beliefs, we will never, under any circumstances, perform or participate in a wedding or marriage ceremony – religious, church, or civil – where a man marries another man or a woman marries another woman. We will also not associate ourselves with any church, minister, Pastor, denomination, fellowship, ministry, or outreach that supports or endorses homosexual marriage.[182]

We are commanded not to have anything to do with the "fruitless deeds of darkness." Rather than fellowship and join with them, we are told to "expose them." If they don't bring the godly doctrine of Christ, we are not to allow them into our homes or we will become partakers with them of their evil deeds. No doubt, this is the height of apostasy and rebellion – that ministers from a "church" can officiate or solemnize a marriage between two men or two women when the Lord clearly states that such an act is an abomination[183] to Him! The Lord Himself will oppose all such ministers to their face.

---

[181] See 2 Corinthians 6:14-15.
[182] See Ephesians 5:11-12; 2 Corinthians 6:14-17; Hebrews 13:4; and 2 John 1:9-11.
[183] The word "abomination" is the strongest word in the English language for hatred. God really detests and hates homosexuality.

The writer of Hebrews said that "marriage must be honored by all." There is no doubt that gay weddings and gay marriages completely dishonor and pervert the holy institution of marriage. Homosexuality defiles the marriage bed, and God warns in the same sentence that He will personally judge all adulterers and all who are sexually immoral. Jesus Himself converts the "bed of sex" to the "bed of sickness."[184] The beds in our homes are different from the beds in the hospitals. Jesus casts the sexually immoral into beds of sickness as punishment for their refusal to repent.

Some of the worst offenders within Christendom are those who are heterosexuals but give approval to homosexual lifestyles and marriages. Paul told the Romans that those who "approve of those who practice" homosexuality deserve God's judgment and death. It is a fearful thing to fall into the hands of the living God. Multitudes of compromising Christians in all denominations and fellowships are accepting homosexual marriages as agreeable and suitable in God's eyes. This is particularly true among the younger generations. Paul was correct when he wrote that in the last days, some would follow "deceiving spirits" and "doctrines of demons."

I write this without hesitation and with full conviction – I would gladly go to jail rather than officiate or attend a homosexual marriage ceremony. For me to endorse such marriages would surely incur the judgment of God in my life. I, even now, personally and publicly repudiate all denominations, churches, ministers, and organizations that perform any marriage between two men or two women. And may the Lord rebuke all judges and civil officials that perform homosexual unions for state or federal governments.

Regarding the Nature of Homosexuality

We believe that homosexuality is a sin and part of the fallen, Adamic nature of mankind. Homosexuality is idolatrous and lustful; that is, homosexual men and lesbian women have rejected God and His truth and have embraced a lie. They are

---

[184] See Revelation 2:21-23.

worshipping the creation (human body), rather than the Creator, who is blessed forevermore.[185]

I am a sinner and so are you. Everyone has sinned against God in thought, word, and deed. Paul wrote that both "Jews and Gentiles" are all under sin. There is no one righteous, no, not even one. There is no one who does good, not even one. When Adam sinned, he plunged the entire human race into sin and rebellion. It was through Adam that sin entered the world.

Homosexuality is a sin against Almighty God. This is the difference between everything that the culture is telling us and what the Bible teaches. The world calls homosexuality good; the Bible calls it evil; the world says it is light; the Bible says it is darkness; the world claims that the fruit is sweet; the Bible claims that the fruit is bitter.[186] Fundamentally, the world doesn't hate us, it hates the Lord because He has declared that its deeds are evil. When we align ourselves with Jesus, the world will hate us too.

Because homosexuals and lesbians have rejected the Lord and His truth, they have exchanged the truth of God for a lie. Rather than worship the Creator, they worship His creation. Rather than walk in love, they walk in lust. For these reasons, God has personally given over homosexuals and lesbians to "uncleanness, vile passions and a depraved mind." Rather than honor the Lord, they dishonor their bodies. God is great and must be greatly praised.

We believe that because of this idolatry, God has given homosexuals over to uncleanness (impurity), vile (shameful) passions, and a depraved (corrupt) mind. That is, God has given homosexuals up to the lusts of their own hearts to dishonor and degrade their bodies with one another.[187]

Throughout Scriptures – both Old Testament and New Testament – idolatry and immorality go together. Wherever people worship idols, they will practice sexual immorality. Balaam taught Balak how to seduce the Israelites through the

---

[185] See Genesis 3:1-6; Romans 3:9; and Romans 1:23-27.
[186] See Isaiah 5:20.
[187] See Romans 1:24-28; Jude 1:7; and Ephesians 4:17-19.

worship of false gods that lead to sexual immorality. Jezebel introduced idolatry and sexual immorality into the church at Thyatira. The early church apostles taught "to abstain from food sacrificed to idols and from sexual immorality."[188] In one verse Paul could say "Do not be idolaters," and in the very next verse write, "Do not commit sexual immorality."[189] Right after Israel made the golden calf, they "rose up and played" with the women in sexual immorality.

Paul teaches in Romans, Chapter 1, that the root cause of homosexuality is idolatry. They have rejected the Creator God and made a god to suit their own imaginations. Rather than run after the Creator, they run after the creation. Rather than embrace Jesus, they embrace one another's body. They reject the love of God and accept the lust of the body. This is a great darkness.

The apostle Jude warned us that the homosexuals of "Sodom and Gomorrah gave themselves up to sexual immorality and perversion. They serve as an example of those who suffer the punishment of eternal fire." The Genesis account describes these homosexuals as "exceedingly wicked men who were sinning greatly against the Lord."[190] It is a frightening thing when someone has been given over to a sin. This is true bondage and addiction.

I remember years ago when I went to San Francisco with my family. Because of some construction on a major road, we had to take a detour to get us to the right freeway. Unfortunately, we turned onto a street filled with homosexual bath houses. We briefly saw 15-20 shirtless men on the sidewalk jumping on each other in unbridled lust. It was such a terrible scene for me, my wife, and my daughter, that I drove out of there as quickly as possible. What Paul said was true: "Having lost all sensitivity, they have given themselves over to sensuality so as to indulge in every kind of impurity, with a continual lust for more."[191]

From the beginning, God created us "male and female." At our core, we are sexual beings. We were created to enjoy sex, but the devil and man have corrupted its original purpose. God

---

[188] See Acts 15:29.
[189] See 1 Corinthians 10:7-8.
[190] See Genesis 13:13.
[191] See Ephesians 4:19 in the NIV translation.

created very sophisticated bodies to love, but we have degraded these bodies to lust.

We maintain that homosexuality is an abomination (detestable) in the eyes of God. It is a sin that must be repented of and that no practicing homosexual can inherit the kingdom of God. [192]

You do not need to be a Hebrew scholar to understand this verse from the Lord: "Do not practice homosexuality, having sex with another man as with a woman. This is a detestable sin." Another translation calls it "an abomination." Yes, there are other abominations, but that does not minimize the gravity of this sin. Leviticus then follows up that verse with a verse describing the punishment for such behavior: "If a man practices homosexuality, having sex with another man as with a woman, both men have committed an abomination (detestable act). They must both be put to death, for they are guilty of a capital offense." This is serious language. You do not need any further training in biblical interpretation to understand what these verses are saying.

Paul warned us, not once, but twice, that no practicing homosexuality could enter the kingdom of God. In fact, he calls such people, "wicked." He writes, "Do you not know that the wicked will not inherit the kingdom of God? Do not be deceived: Neither the sexually immoral nor idolaters nor adulterers nor male prostitutes nor *homosexuals* nor thieves nor the greedy nor drunkards nor slanderers nor swindlers will inherit the kingdom of God." Paul writes emphatically to the Galatian church: "I warn you, as I did before, that those who live like this will not inherit the kingdom of God." What were they doing? "Adultery, sexual immorality, impurity, lewdness, and orgies." A great percentage of the "works of the flesh" are sex sins.

Let me reiterate: No practicing homosexual can inherit the kingdom of God.

Because of the above beliefs, we maintain that homosexuality is not a sexual orientation, but a sexual

---

[192] See Genesis 13:13; Leviticus 18:22; Leviticus 20:13; and 1 Corinthians 6:9-10.

perversion. Homosexuals advocate "safe sex" through condoms; we advocate "holy living" through abstinence. It is not a protected civil right; rather, it is sexual immorality and a deviant sexual behavior that must not be singled out for protection by any laws of our Constitution or any Civil Rights legislation.[193]

I'm amazed at how the liberal media and people living in darkness give new words to deviant behavior. "Fornicators" are now people who are "sexually active." "Sodomites" are now "gays." "Vice," "depravity," and "perversion" are now "sexual orientation." Christians are never described as "pro-life," but "anti-abortion." We are not people who stand up for the "truth," but are "anti-gay," "homophobic," and "hatemongers." What was once "abnormal" is now "normal." What is "unnatural" is now "natural." Somehow, they think that their choice of words tones down the enormity of the sin.

Homosexuality is a sexual perversion. It is an act of immorality. Homosexuality is not an issue of equality, but of morality. It is definitely not a "civil right" that must be protected under our Constitution or any law in our country. Homosexuals are living in utter confusion. Why does the media suppress the truth that homosexuals have much higher incidences of suicide, depression, and sexually transmitted diseases? Jesus was right when He said, "Men love darkness rather than light, because their deeds are evil. Everyone practicing evil hates the light and does not come to the light, lest their deeds should be exposed."[194]

Condoms do not make sex safe. The only safety is to obey the Lord and do His will. He protects those who live right. When we commit sexual immorality, we are unprotected. Unseen curses come into our lives. Someone once said that we are males by birth, but we are men by choice. Be a man! Repent of homosexuality. Reject the feminine voice. Quit feeling sorry for yourself. You're not a woman; you're a man!

---

[193] See 1 Timothy 1:9-10; Leviticus 18:22, 20:13; and Romans 1:26-27.
[194] See John 3:19-20.

Regarding Gay "Christians" & Pro-Gay Theology

We believe that any person who claims to be a practicing Christian and practicing homosexual (gay Christian) at the same time is deceived, disobeying the clear teachings of Scripture, living in darkness, or simply lost in his sins. True Christians have died to sin; how can we live in it any longer? If such a person has escaped the corruption of the world by knowing our Lord and Savior Jesus Christ and is again entangled in it and overcome, he is worse off at the end than he was at the beginning.[195]

The Apostle Paul was very frank and forthright. He told the Romans, "Shall we continue to sin that grace may abound? Certainly not! How shall we who died to sin live any longer in it?" With similar boldness, the Apostle John wrote, "If we say that we have fellowship with Him (the Lord), and walk in darkness, we lie and do not practice the truth. If we say that we have no sin, we deceive ourselves, and the truth is not in us." If we don't "do the Word" of God, we are "deceiving ourselves" and building our lives upon sand.

If a Christian proclaims and receives Jesus as Lord, then he needs to "walk in Him." The "solid foundation of God stands" on this truth – "Let everyone who names the name of Christ depart from evil (wickedness)."[196] To "name the name of Christ" is to be identified as a Christian believer. You are telling others that you are a follower of Christ. How is it possible for a "Christian" man to sleep with another man? This is a corruption of God's original design. No one can live in peace with God who is having sex with someone of the same sex. This is darkness, not light.

Incredibly, the Apostle Peter has declared that Christians are "partakers of the divine nature." The reason this has happened is because we've "escaped the corruption that is in the world through lust." Lust, especially sexual lust, is corrupting this world!

---

[195] See Romans 6:2; 2 Peter 2:20-22; James 1:22-24; 1 John 1:6; and 1 Corinthians 6:9-10.

[196] See 2 Timothy 2:19.

Then a short while later, in this same letter, Peter says that if we have "escaped the pollutions of the world through the knowledge of the Lord and Savior Jesus Christ, and then are again entangled in them and overcome, the latter end is worse for them than the beginning." It actually would have been better if they had not known Christ, than to know Him and then turn away from God's holy commands. It is like a dog returning to its own vomit, and like a pig, having been washed, to jump back into the mud.

There were plenty of homosexuals in Corinth. And Paul said that they got "washed, sanctified, and justified in the name of the Lord Jesus and by the Spirit of God." This happened because they repented, confessed Christ, and took up their cross and followed Him. You can't go back to your old homosexual lifestyle. You can't get "entangled" again. Many former homosexuals who have been set free by Jesus have gone back.

We believe that no one who lives or abides in Christ keeps on living in homosexuality (or any other sin). And no one who continues practicing homosexuality has either seen Him or known Him. If the so-called "gay Christian" says, "I know Christ," but does not do what He commands, he is a liar, and the truth is not in Him.[197]

John said, "He who says, 'I know Him,' and does not keep His commandments, is a liar, and the truth is not in him." Obedience is proof that we know Him. It's also proof that we love Him. "If you love Me, keep My commandments," Jesus said. If we are "born of God," or "born again," then we don't continue on in our sins.

I have some simple questions for those "Christians" who have embraced the homosexual lifestyle or who are heterosexuals, but approve of homosexuality – Name one verse in the Bible that clearly supports homosexual marriage? Name one God-honoring, God-fearing man in the Bible who was also a homosexual? Name one homosexual apostle, prophet, priest, or king? The truth is you cannot name one because there aren't any! If it was God's will, then it would be clearly revealed.

---

[197] See 1 John 2:4 and 3:9.

> *We maintain that no human being is born homosexual nor does God make anyone homosexual. We believe people embrace the homosexual lifestyle by deliberate choice and willful decision and not because of some external condition or genetic predisposition. People give themselves over to this sin.*[198]

I pointed out in first chapter of this book, *The Homosexual Christian?*, that most of the researchers that concluded that homosexuality is somehow genetic, are homosexuals themselves. No one has ever discovered the "gay gene." Drs. Dean Hamer, Simon LeVay, and Richard Pillard have all done research to "prove" the genetic origins of homosexuality. None of them have proved it. And no other researcher has been able to duplicate any of the conclusions of these three homosexuals. Amazingly and deceptively, *Time* magazine announced a cover story entitled *Born Gay: Science Finds a Genetic Link*. Many other scientists have shown that this conclusion is totally false. However, these words get into the national consciousness and it's difficult for the average person to separate truth from fiction.

The sad truth is that God gives homosexuals what they want. He gives them over to their sin. They really are burning in lust for one another. By willful decision and deliberate choice, they chose this lifestyle.

I remember reading through the book *The Mayor of Castro Street: The Life and Times of Harvey Milk*. Milk has been the poster child for the homosexual movement ever since he was elected to public office as the mayor of the Castro District in San Francisco. He was eventually killed, along with San Francisco Mayor George Moscone, by Dan White. It was difficult to read through the book because in page after page we read the stories of his burning lust for younger men (many different men). He was a life-long sex addict; yet, he's always portrayed in the media as some great man. There's even a Harvey Milk High School in New York designed for "gays, lesbians, bisexual, and transgender" teens, and any others who are "questioning their sexuality." Harvey Milk was not a hero; he was a pervert.

---

[198] See Romans 1:24-28; Genesis 13:13; and Jude 1:7.

CHAPTER 6: *A Christian Manifesto on Homosexuality*

We maintain, contrary to pro-gay theology, that King David and Jonathan were heterosexual men who were married to wives and fathered children. Their relationship in the Scriptures was a simple expression of a normal, healthy relationship between two godly men who loved and cared deeply for each other. King David and Jonathan were never involved together in any homosexual activity.[199]

One of the most wicked things that pro-gay Christians and homosexuals have done is to assert that King David and Jonathan were homosexual lovers. It should not surprise us that people living in perversion would pervert the Scripture. There are many who twist the Scriptures to get it to say what they want it to say. A lie can never be the truth.

Both King David and Jonathan were married men. Both fathered children, especially David. Anyone who reads the Bible narrative closely will see that they spent very little time together. David had many wives. David's father (Jesse) and Jonathan's father (Saul) were also men who married women and fathered many children. There was no homosexuality in either family line. David at one point even had ten concubines.

When David lamented Jonathan's death in 2 Samuel, it was not a declaration of homosexual love, but a statement of long-term friends who loved each other in the Lord. Both men feared the Lord. Both men were warriors in Israel. They were fierce fighting men who could easily kill a multitude of enemy forces at a given moment. Surely, no soldier in Israel would have followed a homosexual king. King David was an extraordinary military leader who commanded the respect of his men in the field.

We maintain, contrary to pro-gay theology, that Sodom and Gomorrah were not destroyed because of a lack of hospitality or some environmental disaster, but because of homosexuality and perversion. We also maintain that this destruction by the judgment and wrath of God stands as a biblical and historical truth and example of how God will deal with any individual, family, community, state, or nation that embraces homosexuality and refuses to humble itself and

---

[199] See 2 Samuel 1:26, 3:2-5; 1 Chronicles 3:1-9; 1 Samuel 18:1-4; 1 Samuel 20:17; 2 Samuel 4:4, 9:1-7, 21:7; and 1 Chronicles 8:34, 9:40.

repent. We also believe that it was the Lord Almighty, the only true God, and not the devil, who destroyed Sodom and Gomorrah and the surrounding cities.[200]

I recently heard a popular Christian radio station explain that God destroyed Sodom and Gomorrah because of their lack of hospitality and disregard for the poor (based on an obscure verse in Ezekiel, Chapter 16). The overwhelming testimony of Scripture is that Sodom and Gomorrah were destroyed by the Lord God Almighty for their homosexuality and wickedness.

Consider this language from the Bible: "The LORD destroyed Sodom and Gomorrah," "the LORD rained brimstone and fire on Sodom and Gomorrah, from the LORD out of the heavens. So God overthrew those cities, all the plain, all the inhabitants of the cities, and what grew on the ground," "the whole land is brimstone, salt, and burning, like the overthrow of Sodom and Gomorrah, Admah, and Zeboiim, which the LORD overthrew in His anger and His wrath," "God overthrew Sodom and Gomorrah," "God overthrew Sodom and Gomorrah and their neighbors," "the punishment is greater than the punishment of the sin of Sodom, which was overthrown in a moment, with no hand to help her," "God overthrew Sodom and Gomorrah," "on the day that Lot went out of Sodom it rained fire and brimstone from heaven and destroyed them all," "God turned the cities of Sodom and Gomorrah into ashes, condemned them to destruction, making them an example to those who afterward would live ungodly," and "as Sodom and Gomorrah, and the cities around them are set forth by God as an example, suffering the vengeance of eternal fire."

God is the One who brought this judgment and destruction, not the devil. Even today, any city, state, nation, or government that accepts homosexuality is on the sure path of destruction.

---

[200] See Genesis 13:10, 19:13, 19:24, 19:28-29; Deuteronomy 29:23-24; Isaiah 13:19; Jeremiah 50:40; Amos 4:11; Luke 17:29; 2 Peter 2:6-9; Jude 1:7; and Psalm 11:6.

CHAPTER 6: *A Christian Manifesto on Homosexuality*

Regarding a True Christian's Attitude & Response Toward Homosexuals

We maintain that true Christian believers are to love homosexuals with the love of Christ. We are to pray for them, help them in their need, assist them in their sickness (ex: AIDS), bless them when they curse us, and do everything possible to show them the compassionate love of God.[201]

God is love and His believers will show that love to others. If we are commanded to love our enemies, then surely, we can love homosexuals with the love of Christ. The greatest commandment is to love God and love our neighbor. The new commandment is to love others with the same love Jesus has toward us. The only debt we should carry is the continuing debt to love one another.

We are commanded to bless those who curse us, pray for those who despitefully use us, and do good to those who hate us. This is not easy, but it's what keeps us from becoming bitter. God loves the whole world and gave His Son to demonstrate that love. This is true agape love – Christ died for us.

Christians are to feed the hungry, give drink to the thirsty, take in the stranger, clothe the naked, visit the sick, and go to those in prison. When you do this for others, you are doing it to Jesus. This is profound truth. You'll know how submitted you are to God when you practice these things daily.

All Christians can start by praying for homosexuals and lesbians. Pray for their salvation. Pray for their deliverance. Pray for the scales to fall from their eyes. Pray for their repentance. While not a homosexual, Lot was delivered from Sodom's destruction by the intercession of Abraham. If we don't pray for them, they will never escape. Is it not a revealing message to us that all the homosexual men in Sodom were blind when fire and brimstone rained down from God in heaven?

We maintain that because of the Lord's commandment to love, all true Christian believers will speak the truth in love

---

[201] See Matthew 5:43-46; Leviticus 19:18; Matthew 25:35-40; and Romans 13:8-10.

and seek to bring homosexuals to repentance and to restoration of a right relationship with God through Jesus Christ.[202]

Speaking the truth in love is not as easy as it sounds. The wisdom of God teaches that open rebuke is better than secret love. Too many of us live in the fear of man. The only one we should fear is God. We are so worried about not offending that we say nothing. Regarding homosexuality, we cannot be silent. The Lord Jesus spoke to Paul in a night vision: "Do not be afraid, but speak, and do not keep silent."[203] How will homosexuals ever "call on Him" and "believe in Him" if they never hear from us? Speak the truth in love!

God is commanding all men – not just homosexuals – to repent. Why is repentance so necessary? Because God has appointed a day – the great Day of the Lord – in which He will judge the world in righteousness by the One He has chosen, Jesus Christ the Lord. On Judgment Day, it will be too late. This is the only reason Jesus is delaying His coming. God wants all men to repent because God wants all men to be saved.[204] He also wants all men to come to the knowledge of the truth. Salvation is just the beginning. We must grow in the grace and knowledge of Jesus Christ our Lord.

So who really loves the homosexual? Is it those approving of their sinful lifestyle or those who are telling them the truth? I know this sounds harsh, but it's true – those living as homosexuals and lesbians who do not repent will be thrown into the lake of fire. If we truly love them, we will warn them of the coming wrath. Those who die in their sins will perish forever.

The first word of the gospel and the first word to the homosexual is not love, grace, or mercy. It is "repent." All of us must repent.

We will do everything in our power to help any man or woman who wants to leave the homosexual lifestyle and assist

---

[202] See Ephesians 4:15; Acts 17:30-31; Mark 1:15; Hebrews 6:1.
[203] See Acts 18:9.
[204] See 2 Peter 3:9 and 1 Timothy 2:4.

CHAPTER 6: *A Christian Manifesto on Homosexuality*

other ministries, agencies, and counseling centers that do the same.[205]

The power of the gospel of Jesus Christ really works to transform the lives of any sinner. Jesus changes people. When you become a Christian, God's Spirit will live in you and you will be changed. This is the glorious hope of those who have come into Christ.

This is a sobering truth: Anyone living as a homosexual will go to hell when he dies. However, no Christian should declare that truth without a willingness to do everything in his power to make sure that doesn't happen. For this reason, Christians should do whatever it takes to help someone who is struggling with same-sex attraction.

Historically, our church has assisted many ministries and agencies that help people get out of the homosexual lifestyle. We've helped with finances, prayer, resources, and manpower. Even as I write this teaching, we are preparing next month to help in significant ways the main ministry in our city that reaches out to homosexuals and lesbians. We are behind them 100%.

In just the last few months, I have personally talked one on one with homosexuals and lesbians and strongly encouraged them to get out of relationships or to get professional counseling from Christian ministries. I will continue to do this outreach as long as the Lord lets me live.

We reject the foolish "God hates fags" position of some Christian groups. Because of the command to love our enemies, the greatest commandment, John 3:16, and the fruit of the Spirit, this attitude and belief cannot be tolerated or accepted.[206]

Pastor Fred Phelps (1929-2014) established Westboro Baptist Church in 1955 in Topeka, Kansas. They are well-known for their campaign of "God hates fags." They even host the dark website, www.godhatesfags.com. They also protest in various places around our country with posters and signs that read: "Thank God for AIDS," "Fags burn in Hell," "God hates America," and

---

[205] See Acts 17:4, 18:4, 19:26, and 26:28. Paul was constantly "persuading" people to the truth. We should do the same.
[206] See Matthew 5:43-46, 22:37-40; John 3:16, Galatians 5:22-23.

"Thank God for Dead Soldiers." At the time of this writing, they claim to have held over 55,000 demonstrations.

All Christians (everyone actually) should reject this foolish and hateful group. Here are people supposedly saved by God's love and grace, preaching *only* God's hatred and wrath.

This "church" reminds me of the actions of the apostles James and John in Luke, Chapter 9. When a Samaritan village didn't receive Jesus, these two brothers asked the Lord if they could call down fire from heaven like Elijah did. They wanted to burn up these Samaritans for their rejection of Jesus! The Lord immediately corrects their attitude. He says, "You don't know what spirit you are of." In other words, Jesus said that a "spirit" was emanating from them that they didn't even realize. It was a spirit of anger and judgment.

Then Jesus adds these powerful words: "For the Son of Man did not come to destroy men's lives but to save them." In our dispensation of grace, Jesus is the SAVIOR, not the DESTROYER. This truth is affirmed by Jesus in the verse right after the famous John 3:16. Verse 17 reads, "For God did not send His Son into the world to condemn the world, but that the world through Him might be saved." It's not about condemnation, but salvation. Jesus came to "seek and to save lost people," not to "seek and to destroy" them. Paul told Timothy that "this is a faithful saying and worthy of all acceptance, that Christ Jesus came into the world to save sinners, of whom I am the worst."[207]

The greatest commandment in the Bible is to love God and to love our neighbor. How can you say, "I love God," and hate your neighbor? If you can't love your fellow man whom you can see, you cannot love God whom you cannot see. James asked how is it possible to have blessing and cursing coming out of the same mouth? So often, we bless God but curse man (who is made in the image and likeness of God).

Here is what I would ask the Westboro Church: Why does God our Father send rain on both the just and unjust. Why does He let the sun shine on the evil and the righteous? If we only love those that love us, we are doing no better than the tax collectors and sinners. Jesus made the startling statement in Luke 6:35-36,

---

[207] See Luke 19:10 and 1 Timothy 1:15.

that His Father (and ours) "is kind to the ungrateful and wicked. Be merciful, just as our Father is merciful."[208] God is kind to the wicked. How? Because He lets them live another day without destroying them. He's giving them more time to repent and be saved.

The fruit of the Spirit is love. Our continuing debt is to love one another. If we don't love, we are a clanging cymbal and good for nothing. The sad reality for the Westboro Church believers is that if they don't love, it's proof that they don't know God for God is love.[209]

Regarding Jesus Christ and the Salvation of Homosexuals

We maintain that the only true healing, deliverance, and salvation for a homosexual from his sin is through the Lord and Savior Jesus Christ, the Son of God.[210]

The only person who can set a homosexual free from his sin is the Lord Jesus Christ. When Jesus sets you free, you will be free indeed. There are no other saviors, gods, or deliverers who can break the power of sin over our lives. There is only one Mediator between God and man – the Man Jesus Christ. The apostle Peter made this powerful declaration in Acts 4:12, "Salvation is found in no one else, for there is no other name under heaven given to men by which we must be saved." What is that name? Peter said it was "Jesus Christ of Nazareth."

When Paul was talking about a man's struggle with the power of sin in Romans, Chapter 7, he said that the very things that he hated were the things that he did, and the things that he wanted to do were the things he did not do. He realized that if his own desires were being violated, then it was not him but "sin living in me." And what did Paul say was the answer to the man

---

[208] Incidentally, nearly all the verses in Luke 6:27-38 have Greek imperative verbs of command. Jesus is commanding us to love our enemies, those who hate us, and those who despitefully use us. There are no other options.
[209] See Galatians 5:22; Romans 13:10; 1 Corinthians 13:1-3; and 1 John 4:8.
[210] See John 8:36; Romans 7:24-25; Acts 4:12; 1 Timothy 2:5; and 1 John 5:12.

trapped in such a predicament? How does anyone get out from under the power of sin? Who would rescue and deliver Paul from this "body of death?" He gives the only answer: "I thank God – through Jesus Christ our Lord! Jesus is not the trivial answer; He is the only answer!

Jesus Christ came into this world as Savior of the world. He is the Savior not only of my sins, but the sins of the whole world. As one evangelist friend told me: "I am a sinner; I need a Savior; my Savior is Jesus Christ." Is your Savior, Jesus Christ?

I appreciate good counselors. I appreciate Pastors who take time to walk people through their problems and troubles. Thank God for friends who can support us in our time of anguish and difficulty. None of these people's valuable contributions should be discounted.

However, the only true deliverer for mankind is the Lord Jesus Christ. Everything else is a substitute. No man can break the power of sin off of your life. Only God can do that. Jesus Christ is Lord and God, and He is the Lord Almighty that can deliver you from homosexual bondage.

We believe that any non-believer, including the homosexual, can inherit the kingdom of God, receive eternal life, and be washed, sanctified, and justified by God's Spirit by repentance from his sins and believing, trusting, and confessing Jesus Christ as his Lord and Savior.[211]

The only way any person can be saved and receive eternal life is by believing in the Lord Jesus Christ, repenting of and confessing his sins, and believing that God the Father raised Him from the dead. No one can get into heaven except through the Lord Jesus Christ. Jesus stated plainly in John 6:47, "Most assuredly I say to you, he who believes in Me has everlasting life." Jesus also said in John 11:25, "I am the resurrection and the life. He who believes in Me, though he may die, he shall live."

If you are a homosexual today, you can be changed. You can be "washed, sanctified, and justified" by God's Spirit. You can be given new desires and a new life. True living is not having

---

[211] See 1 Corinthians 6:9-11; Romans 10:9-13; John 3:36 and John 6:40.

sex with another man; it is having a personal relationship with Jesus Christ. He is life – eternal life.

Homosexuality is a sin that must be repented of. To die living in homosexuality is to die in your sins and go to an eternal hell. There is something far better – peace with God!

In Summary

Let's summarize what we have declared in this Christian Manifesto on Homosexuality.
- The only marriage accepted and approved by God is between one man and one woman. "One wife for life." For Christian believers, we are only to marry other Christians.
- Homosexuality is a sin. There is no "gay gene." Men and women give themselves over to this sin by deliberate choice.
- No practicing homosexual "Christian" will inherit the kingdom of God. If you die living in the homosexual lifestyle, you will not enter heaven.
- Christian believers are to love homosexuals with the love of Christ. This means that we are to tell them the truth about homosexuality and warn them of its dangers.

The only salvation for the homosexual (and any sinner) is through the Lord Jesus Christ. No one can break the power of sin over our lives except Jesus Christ. He is the only Savior and only Mediator.

Selected Bibliography
(By Author)

Bauckham, Richard J., *Word Biblical Commentary: 2 Peter and Jude*, Word Books Publishers, Waco, Texas.

Blomberg, Craig, *1 Corinthians*, The NIV Application Commentary, Zondervan Publishing House, Grand Rapids, Michigan.

Blum, Edwin, *The Expositor's Bible Commentary: Jude*, Zondervan Publishing House, Grand Rapids, Michigan.

Bray, Gerald, *Ancient Commentary on Scripture, New Testament, Volume VI, Romans*, Inter-Varsity Press, Downers Grove, Illinois.

Bray, Gerald, *Ancient Commentary on Scripture, New Testament, Volume VII, 1-2 Corinthians*, Inter-Varsity Press, Downers Grove, Illinois.

Bruce, F. F., *Romans*, Revised Edition, Tyndale New Testament Commentaries, Eerdmans Publishing Company, Grand Rapids, Michigan.

Carter, David, *Stonewall*: The Riots that Sparked the Gay Revolution, St. Martin's Press, New York, New York. (This is a non-Christian book. It is listed here for the important historical information on the Stonewall riots that took place in Greenwich Village in New York City).

Conner, Kevin J., *The Epistle of Jude: An Exposition*, Kevin Conner, KJC Publications, Vermont, Victoria, Australia.

Conner, Kevin J., *The Epistle to the Romans*, A Commentary, City Bible Publishing, Portland, Oregon.

Cranfield, C. E. B., *Romans: A Shorter Commentary*, Eerdmans Publishing Company, Grand Rapids, Michigan.

Dallas, Joe, *Desires in Conflict*, Harvest House Publishers, Eugene, Oregon.

Davies, Bob & Rentzel, Lori, *Coming Out of Homosexuality*: New Freedom for Men and Men, InterVarsity Press, Downers Grove, Illinois.

Edwards, James R., *Romans*, New International Biblical Commentary, Hendrickson Publishers, Peabody, Massachusetts.

Fee, Gordon D., *1 and 2 Timothy, Titus*, New International Biblical Commentary, Hendrickson Publishers, Peabody, Massachusetts.

Guthrie, Donald, *The Pastoral Epistles*, Revised Edition, Tyndale New Testament Commentaries, Eerdmans Publishing Company, Grand Rapids, Michigan.

Haley, Mike, *101 Frequently Asked Questions About Homosexuality*, Harvest House Publishers, Eugene, Oregon.

Hamer, Dean and Peter Copeland, *The Science of Desire*, Simon and Schuster, New York, New York. (This is a non-Christian book).

Hiebert, D. Edmond, *First Timothy*, Everyman's Commentary, Moody Press, Chicago, Illinois.

Konrad, Jeff, *You Don't Have to be Gay*: Hope and Freedom for Males Struggling With Homosexuality or For Those Who Know Someone Who Is, Pacific Publishing House, Hilo, Hawaii.

LeVay, Simon, *The Sexual Brain*, MIT Press, Cambridge, Massachusetts. (This is a non-Christian book).

Lewis, C. S., *The Problem of Pain*, HarperOne Publishers, San Francisco, California.

Bibliography

McIlhenny, Chuck & Donna and Frank York, *When the Wicked Seize a City*: A Grim Look at the Future and a Warning to the Church, Huntington House Publishers, Lafayette, Louisiana.

Moo, Douglas, *The NIV Application Commentary on 2 Peter and Jude*, Zondervan Publishing House, Grand Rapids, Michigan.

Newman, B. W. and E. A. Nida, *A Handbook on Paul's Letter to the Romans*, United Bible Society (UBS) translators.

Phillips, John, *Exploring Romans*, Moody Press, Chicago, Illinois.

Prior, David, *The Message of 1 Corinthians*, The Bible Speaks Today, Inter-Varsity Press, Downers Grove, Illinois.

Shilts, Randy, *The Mayor of Castro Street*: The Life and Times of Harvey Milk, St. Martin's Press, New York, New York. (This is a book written by a non-Christian author and is listed here because of its important historical background on the most famous homosexual in American history (Harvey Milk). Shilts was a homosexual journalist who died of AIDS in 1994).

Soards, Marion L., *1 Corinthians*, New International Biblical Commentary (NIBC), Hendrickson Publishers, Peabody, Massachusetts.

Stott, John, *Romans: God's Good News for the World*, Inter-Varsity Press, Downers Grove, Illinois.

Strauch, Alexander, *Biblical Eldership*: An Urgent Call to Restore Biblical Church Leadership, Second Edition, Lewis and Roth Publishers, Littleton, Colorado.

Wiersbe, Warren, *Be Right: Romans*, The BE Series Commentary, David C. Cook Publishers.

Scriptural Reference Index

Genesis
1:27   17, 18
1:28   124
Chap 1-2 14, 19
2:24   122, 123
3:1-6   128
3:5-6   79
Chap 3   14
Chap 4   114
5:1-2   18
6:2   28
6:6   28
Chap 6   28
Chap 7   38
9:1   124
9:7   124
10:19   28
13:10   28, 40, 45, 136
13:10-12 36
13:13   45, 129, 130, 134
14:2   28
14:8   28
14:12   36
Chap 14   45
15:16   41
18:20-21 45
18:23-25 34
Chap 18   34
19:1   29, 46
19:4   46
19:4-5   28, 29
19:5   29, 46
19:7   36, 46
19:8   46
19:10   46
19:11   46
19:12   46
19:13   40, 45, 136
19:15   46
19:16   46
19:22-23 28
19:24   30, 40, 136
19:26   47
19:27-28 33
19:28-29 136
19:29   40, 47
19:30   28
19:30-38 36
Chap 19   27, 28, 29, 32, 38, 42, 57, 104
24:16   124, 125

Exodus
21:16   115
21:17   114

Leviticus
18:22   7, 9, 57, 88, 119, 130, 131
18:24   9
18:25   9
18:27-29 9
Chap 18   6, 7, 9
19:18   137
20:13   9, 57, 88, 121, 130, 131
Chap 20   6, 7
21:7   13
21:14   124
21:15-16 13

Deuteronomy
18:22   60
22:5   8
22:13-21 125
24:7   115
27:16   114
29:23   27, 40
29:23-24 136

1 Samuel
Chap 13-21 5
Chap 14   5
16:5-10   6
17:12   6
Chap 17   5
18:1   5
18:3   4
18:1-4   135
18:20   5
18:27-28   5
19:11-18   4
Chap 19   5
20:17   4, 135
20:30   4
20:33   4
Chap 21-30 5
23:16-18   5
Chap 30   5
31:2   6
Chap 31   5

2 Samuel
1:1-16   2
1:19   3

1:24-25	3	**Psalms**		50:40	40, 41, 136
1:26	2, 3, 5, 135	11:6	30, 136		
Chap 1	135	19:1-4	75	**Lamentations**	
3:2-5	3, 135	106:14	118	4:6	43
3:7	6	106:15	118		
4:4	4, 135	106:19	80	**Ezekiel**	
9:1-7	4, 135	106:19-22	73	3:18-19	111
21:7	135	106:21-22	80	16:46-49	42
21:8	6	147:5	75	16:48	42
21:11	6			Chap 16	136
		Proverbs		18:23	40
		6:16-19	8	22:26	100
1 Kings		6:30	104	33:8-9	10
5:1	5	10:2	34	33:11	40
22:14	57	11:4	34	44:23	100
22:36	58	11:6	34		
22:38	63	12:22	8	**Hosea**	
Chap 22	53	12:19	57	4:6	100
		19:21	63	11:8	28
1 Chronicles		21:30	62		
2:13-16	6	27:20	105	**Amos**	
3:1-9	3, 135			4:11	40, 42, 136
8:33	6	**Isaiah**			
8:34	4, 135	1:10	42		
9:39	6	3:8-9	42	**Zephaniah**	
9:40	4, 135	3:9	45	2:9	41
10:2	6	5:20	52, 100, 128		
		13:10	40	**Malachi**	
2 Chronicles		13:19	41, 136	2:6	44, 100
18:6	54	14:27	63	2:14	122
18:7	49	40:12	76	2:14-16	18, 124
18:12	56	40:26	76		
18:13	57	40:28	76	**Matthew**	
18:15	57			5:28	104
18:16	58	**Jeremiah**		5:43-46	137, 139
18:19	59	23:9	44		
18:30	62	23:14	44	10:15	37
Chap 18	53	49:17-18	41	10:37	65

11:8 104	17:29 30, 37	**Romans**
11:23-24 37	40, 136	1:16 69
19:4 18	17:30 39	1:17 69, 72
19:4-6 20, 123	17:31-32 47	1:18 69, 70,
22:37-40 139	17:34-36 38	72, 73, 89
23:32 41	17:37 38	1:18-28 67, 77,
24:4 102	19:10 140	117
24:44 39	21:8 102	1:19 72, 73
25:13 39		1:20 72, 74
25:35-40 137	**John**	1:21 73, 75, 77,
25:41 30	3:16 139, 140	80, 90, 91
	3:17 146	1:22 77, 78
Mark	3:19-20 53, 131	1:23 73, 77,
1:15 138	3:36 142	79, 83
6:11 37	6:40 142	1:23-27 128
7:21-23 104	6:47 142	1:24 29, 74,
9:40 50	7:7 53	80, 81, 85,
9:43-48 30	8:36 141	86, 117, 118
10:6 18	8:44 116	1:24-28 128,
10:6-8 1, 19	11:25 142	134
10:6-9 122, 123	12:43 55, 65	1:25 44, 71,
13:32 39	15:18 53	74, 80, 83,
	17:17 108	89, 117
Luke	17:19 108	1:26 29, 74,
1:27 124		80, 85, 86,
6:26 55	**Acts**	117, 118
6:27-38 141	4:12 141	1:26-27 53, 57,
6:35-36 140	7:24 34	67, 82, 85,
7:25 104	13:39 109	98, 117,
9:50 50	15:29 129	118, 119,
Chap 9 140	17:4 139	131
10:12 37	17:30-31 91,	1:27 29, 74,
12:40 39	106, 138	88, 89, 117
12:47-48 43	18:4 139	1:28 29, 71,
16:18 20, 104	18:9 138	73, 77, 90,
16:31 22	19:26 139	118
17:26-29 37	20:27-28 10	1:31 53, 72
17:27 39	26:28 139	1:31-2:2 57
17:28 39		1:32 44

Chap 1	29		130, 132	5:22	141
2:2	53, 71, 73	6:9-11	98, 110,	5:22-23	139
2:8	70		119, 142	6:7	101
2:17-24	113	6:10	100		
Chap 2	71	6:11	106	*Ephesians*	
3:5	70	6:15	99	4:15	138
3:9	128	6:16	99	4:17-19	128
3:20	113	6:19	99	4:18	82
3:24	109	Chap 6	99	4:19	129
4:15	70	7:2	122, 124	5:3	82
5:1	109	7:25	124	5:5	101, 115
5:9	70, 109	7:28	124	5:11-12	91, 126
6:2	132	7:37	124	5:22-23	122
7:2-3	122	7:39	124	5:25	20
7:7-12	113	9:5	123	5:26	108
7:24-25	141	9:13	99	5:30	20
Chap 7	141	9:24	99	5:31	123
8:33-34	109	10:7-8	128	5:32	20
9:21-22	85	11:7-9	18	6:13-14	64
9:22	70	12:1	99		
10:9-13	142	13:1-3	141	*Colossians*	
12:19	70	15:33	101	1:15	74
13:4	70			3:5	82, 85
13:5	70	*2 Corinthians*		3:8	112
13:8-10	137	1:8	99	3:18-19	122
13:10	141	6:14-15	49, 126		
15:16	108	6:14-17	126	*1 Thessalonians*	
		11:2	20	2:16	41
1 Corinthians		11:3	102	3:13	107
1:2	108	12:21	82	4:5	85, 108
3:16	99			4:7	82
5:6	99, 119	*Galatians*		5:23	108
5:9-13	103, 119	2:16	109		
6:2	99	3:24	109	*2 Thessalonians*	
6:3	99	Chap 3	113	2:3	101
6:9	99, 100,	5:17	84	2:11	89
	104, 111, 115,	5:19	82		
	116	5:19-21	101	*1 Timothy*	
6:9-10	57, 95,	5:21	116	1:6-7	112

152

1:8	112	12:14	107	3:9	133
1:9	111, 115	12:16	103, 114	4:8	141
1:9-10	57, 113, 116, 119, 131	13:4	103, 115, 126	5:12	141
1:9-11	98, 111, 113	13:12	108	**2 John**	
1:10	105, 111, 115	**James**		1:9-11	126
1:11	116	1:16	102	**Jude**	
1:15	140	1:22-24	132	1:5	27
1:17	74	3:9	18	1:5-7	27
2:4	138	**1 Peter**		1:6	27, 28, 30
2:5	141	1:16	107	1:7	25, 27, 28, 29, 30, 31, 33, 57, 82, 128, 134, 136
2:14	102	3:1-7	122		
3:1-2	12				
3:2	122	**2 Peter**			
3:4-5	12	2:4	27, 32	1:24	109
3:12	12	2:4-6	32		
5:14	124	2:5	32	**Revelation**	
		2:6	29, 32, 42	1:5-6	107
2 Timothy		2:6-8	31, 57	2:21-23	127
1:9	61	2:6-9	136	2:22	104
2:19	49, 132	2:8	35	9:5	36
2:21	107	2:9	34	9:21	41
3:12	61	2:20-22	132	11:10	36
		3:5-7	32	12:9	102
Titus		3:9	40, 138	14:10	36
1:6	12	3:9-10	106	19:7-8	20
1:9	12			19:17-21	38
1:12	116	**1 John**		20:8	102
3:7	109	1:6	132	20:10	36, 102
		1:7	107	21:2	20
Hebrews		1:9	107	21:8	101, 116
6:1	138	2:4	133	22:15	101
10:10	108	2:22	116		
11:27	74	3:7	102		

Made in the USA
Monee, IL
20 January 2024